STRAIGHT ENOUGH

A Memoir

Lorinda Boyer

STRAIGHT ENOUGH

A Memoir

Lorinda Boyer

Sidekick Press
Bellingham, Washington

This memoir represents the author's recollection of her past. These true stories are faithfully composed based on memory, photographs, diary entries, and other supporting documents. Some names, places, and other identifying details have been changed to protect the privacy of those represented. Conversations between individuals are meant to reflect the essence, meaning, and spirit of the events described.

Published 2021
Printed in the United States of America
ISBN: 978-1-7365358-0-6
LCCN: 2021903114

Sidekick Press
2950 Newmarket Street, Suite 101-329
Bellingham, Washington 98226
sidekickpress.com

Lorinda Boyer, 1971-
Straight Enough: A Memoir

Dedication

Wally, for giving me a reason to dream.
Michelle, for teaching me how to dream.
Sandy, for making my dreams come true.

one

The Bangles belt out *Manic Monday* through my CD Walkman headphones while I hum and bob along, absorbed in a dreamy daze of words and music. I move gradually down the aisle, shelving returned books, entirely oblivious of my coworker, Jason, slinking up behind me. Unable to hear warning sounds of his frenetic panting and the slap of his flip-flops against bare feet, I unknowingly bend over and shove a book into place, leaving my unprotected butt as an open target. He grabs a handful of my jeans and flesh, squeezes hard. I shoot straight up, but before I can pivot to face him, he pulls me into his chest. I suck in my breath. My stomach tightens. Through the thin, slick fabric of his shorts I feel his dick hardening against the small of my back. His sweaty hands fondle my breasts. The stubble of his chin scratches the exposed skin between my neck and shoulder, transporting me instantly to another time and place—to my uncle's bristly chin hair rubbing against a smaller version of me. And just as I did then, I remain paralyzed, immobile, unable to cry for help.

"*Shhh . . .*" Jason whispers into my ear, and I hear my uncle say, "Don't tell anyone, George."

I hated the name, George. It was a boy's name. But my uncle thought he was being funny, and I didn't want to upset him. Grandma and Grandpa's house, or rather, their single-wide mobile home, was our family hub. My uncles, aunts, and cousins all gathered in the confined quarters routinely to visit. We were so crowded that the physical closeness only created a cramped anonymity that allowed me to be in unseen contact with the probing of my uncle's fingers, the rubbing of his knee in my crotch as he swung me up to play "horsey." The sensations tingled in a good way, and it wasn't until I caught a glance of my perpetrator's leering expression or heard him whisper, "Don't tell anyone, George, or bad things will happen," that a darkness fell, and I knew that what we were involved in was shady. And, even though no one said as much, by six years old, I knew this was a wedge between Jesus and me. This was the cross I took up, and at twenty, I carried it still. I'd fallen out of favor with God and he had turned on me.

I shrug the memory away even as the voice inside me warns, "be very quiet." Minutes or maybe only seconds later, Jason releases me, saunters away. When he's entirely out of sight, I exhale. A tremor quakes in my gut, moving slowly, methodically, through my limbs until I no longer feel wholly connected to my body. As a child, I held my breath until the edges of my brain grew fuzzy and the sparkly dust that falls just before unconsciousness danced and floated before my eyes. Sometimes, if I tried hard enough, I fell weightlessly into nothing, enveloped in darkness. But most times, my breath came back in a painful gust of air, sharp enough to make me grab my chest. My ears echo with Jason's threatening, "*shhh*," like air escaping a tire. When I'm able to feel my feet beneath me, I force myself to run to the bathroom at the back of the library. I close the door, lock myself inside. I stare at my reflection in the mirror. *How can this be happening again?* My brownish blonde hair is pulled away from my face in a loose ponytail. My jeans are shapeless, my shirt long-sleeved, nothing figure-hugging, nothing to invite Jason's behavior. Why can't I blend in like other women seem able to?

"You're so pretty," I hear my uncle's voice swelling inside.

I feel him pull me in, swallow me in his grip. I hadn't tried to be pretty. I hadn't tried to be anything. I had simply been a child. But somehow my sinful spirit caused me to fall then as it has now. Why else would Jason think I wanted his attention? I won't dare cry, I must pull myself together, get back to work. There's a light rap at the door, and I hear my mother-in-law's worried voice. She works as interlibrary loan manager in my department. Library jobs are coveted union county jobs, so someone must die or retire for positions to open. But my mother-in-law, Jo, pulled some strings and got me hired. That was six months ago.

"Lorinda, you okay?"

"Yes." I splash cool water on my face, open the door.

I bump directly into Jo's embrace. She's unquestionably a second mother to me, but completely different from mine. Jo is petite, with skinny legs and a backside so pancake-flat she has trouble keeping her stirrup pants from sliding off. Her hair is thinning, and, as a result, she carefully curls and combs what's remaining to minimize her scalp showing through. She has a full smile of dentures she's had since she was quite young. They're a bit too large to allow her lips to fully close, giving her a permanent pout. She's sweet as sugar but also passionately loyal to her family. I married her only son, Chet, upon graduation from high school two years ago.

Jo pulls away, does a quick study of my face, then grasps my hand and leads me to her desk. She sinks into her chair; I lean against one of the bookshelves, facing her.

"Hun, what happened?" she rolls her chair in tighter to me.

Nothing! I know better than to speak, silence is my savior.

Jo reaches up, brushes a stray hair from my eye. This simple, loving gesture unlocks something inside, and I shock myself by doing something I never could do as a child—I blurt out what happened. I let it tumble out of my mouth in one rushed sentence, "Jasongrabbedmeandfeltmeup."

Jo's expression of shock morphs into rage. She leaps from her desk, knocking her chair over, and storms away. I slide down the bookcase, watching as she marches to the director's office. Oh God, what have I done? I wrap my arms tight around me. I can't imagine what she's saying to the director behind closed doors. I'm embarrassed, terrified. I want to disappear. What if he's angry with me? My stomach roils with regret. Will I lose my job?

"Oh God, forgive me," I pray.

Finally, the director opens his door, motions for me to come in. My legs tremble, but I stand, will my feet to move, one in front of the other. I desperately hope Jason is nowhere around.

"Lorinda, please sit down." The director points to a chair next to Jo. "Can you tell me in your own words what happened?"

He looks more "fatherly concern" than "stern reprimand," but instinctively I fold in on myself like a flower closing its petals at dusk.

Jo pats me on the knee, "Honey, tell him what you told me."

"*Um*," I fumble, "I don't know . . ." The outburst I had with Jo was uncharacteristic for me and now I can't find the words or the bravery to repeat what I told her.

"Well, understandably, she's upset," Jo cuts in, "but she told me and that should be enough!"

The director sighs and pulls off his glasses.

"Let's do this." He rubs his forehead. "Lorinda, you write down your version of what happened, and I'll have Jason do the same." He replaces his glasses, hands me a blank piece of paper and pen.

"Will that work for you, Jo?" He peers over his lenses at her.

She nods. But *I* don't feel any better. What am I going to write? That a forty-year-old man grabbed my butt and pressed his erection into my back while groping at my breasts? I imagine Jason running his fingers through his sparse wisps of hair, smiling at me over the top of his mirrored sunglasses. I feel nauseous as I write down in as few words as I can what transpired. I shove the paper across the director's desk, and I flee, without a word to him or Jo.

The safest place to hide is in the bookmobile office—nearly always accessible, nearly always devoid of people, with many places to curl up. I choose a spot on the floor between a desk and shelf of new books. I contemplate the books, stiff as soldiers, spines straight, uncracked, and unblemished. I've always loved books. Within their pages I'm easily transported to places I assume

I'll never see, and taken on adventures I figure I'll never have. But I know that all too soon these new volumes will be in the hands of the public. They'll get torn, worn, and broken-down. I inhale their fresh, inky scent while it still floods the small space and close my eyes. I pray for the books, for strength against the unavoidable abuse they'll endure. And, finally, I cry.

Before the end of the week, an anti-sexual-harassment policy is drafted and delivered to each library employee in all twelve of our county's library branches. After reading and signing the policies, we're informed we will also be required to attend a seminar on sexual harassment in the workplace. I may as well have leprosy for the wide berth everyone gives me. The mostly female library staff sneers behind my back at how ludicrous this sexual harassment training is, and I now understand that many of the women around me welcome Jason's advances. Maybe they're even flattered by him. Now I feel conflicted and wonder if maybe I made too big a deal. But I buffer myself with the knowledge that Jo backs me. Even so, no matter how vehemently she argues with the director and library board, the consensus is that the library is doing all it's legally required to do. She's found that the library is more concerned Jason may take legal action against them. Jo's furious, and, as president of the library employees' local union, she appeals to the greater, overseeing state union for guidance. Within days, representatives from the union descend upon our library. But as weeks and then months pass, I begin to feel that my involvement in the issue has taken a back seat to Jo's driving objective to get Jason sacked. This has become her sole mission, to prove that all the fuss has been worth it.

In the interim, I'm required to work with Jason daily, even accompanying him—alone—on book deliveries to Lummi Island Library, which involves taking a ferry. I sit rigid in the front passenger seat, staring straight ahead, and Jason routinely whistles cockily to himself, but we never converse. The silence is a relief, and, at the same time, a terrific source of discomfort. Instinctively, I default to silence, but I fear silence from others as dangerous.

Shortly after the harassment incident, Jason and I go out in the van for a delivery. Before starting up the engine, Jason leans over so closely his shoulder brushes mine. I vault from my seat, recoil, then flatten cartoon-character-like against the door.

"Chill," he hisses, holding out a piece of gum.

I look from him to the gum but don't dare move.

"Whatever." He lets the gum fall to the ground.

I'm embarrassed. My face flushes as I bend to pick it up.

"Sorry," I mumble.

"Meh." Jason smirks. "Sometimes I push the envelope."

I've never heard the expression, but I wonder if he's trying to apologize. I feel stupid, humiliated, and incredibly lonely.

I wish Chet would wrap his arms around me, promise to protect me. Instead, he blames me for the whole incident. He's annoyed, and reprimands me for being too friendly and talkative with men, for leading men on with my smile, which could be mistakenly interpreted as flirting. His jealousy makes him angry, but Jo warns him not to get involved, noting how tense the library atmosphere is already. The stress from Chet's impatience and my coworkers' disdain is emotionally exhausting. I start hating work. I want to quit. Jo assures me she's making progress, that

Jason is as good as fired, but I'm losing hope. I wish now I'd kept my mouth shut; this whole thing totally sucks.

Then, like a miracle dropped directly from heaven, Jason is gone. I show up one morning to find a sign posted on the staff bulletin board. The delivery driver position needs to be filled as Jason has unexpectedly resigned. I'm elated. Maybe I've reestablished favor in the eyes of God after all. God is all-knowing, and therefore, must know how sorry I am about the incident between Jason and me. Maybe this is my sign he hasn't turned his back on me at all. I'm so relieved, I feel like I could fly, but I fight the urge to run through the library screaming, "Yes! Yes!" Because despite my overwhelming sense of liberation, I'm worried my coworkers will blame me. I'm spared from their reactions for the moment, as the responsibility of delivering to the county branches falls temporarily on my shoulders.

With twelve separate library branches, I'll end up traversing a large stretch of the county. At first, I'm afraid I'll get lost. I'm not known for having a keen sense of direction. Though I've lived in Whatcom County all my life, I'm only certain of a handful of road names. Maps remain a complete mystery. Chet drives when we are together, and I rarely pay attention to how we get from one place to another. Even so, I'm relieved to be out alone on the road, so I clumsily navigate my way around.

In the morning, after loading the van, I tune the radio to the local Christian station and head out. I'm aware that Central Services borders between the city limits of Bellingham and the county and that I'm to go north to the Lynden library. The route winds for about fifteen miles in and out of farmland. I never tire of viewing the extensive cornucopia of farm animals, berry crops and hay fields. At the library, I jump from the van and am met by two women pushing book trucks. We pile the boxes onto the carts, wheel them in through the back doors of the library. I load the boxes intended for return to Central Services and then head east to the Sumas Library.

In Sumas, the farms are bigger and the distance between houses is greater. I find myself behind a tractor plodding along at ten miles per hour. Eventually, the road widens, and I pull around. The driver waves and I nod in response. The library shares space with the local seniors' center, and I'm met with the pungent odor of cooked cabbage permeating from the adjoining room. I peek my head around the wall, wave to the gray-haired men and women bent over bowls of soup. Some of them lift their eyes, smiling around their spoons, while others carry on as if they don't see me. And maybe they don't.

Sumas is a tiny town with a tiny library, and I'm in and out quickly. Well ahead of schedule, I look for a place to buy a drink to sip on. I don't like soda, but I pull up to a Dairy Queen; they sell iced tea. The van sits high enough that I'm level with the young woman in the drive-up window. She's alternately chomping and snapping a wad of gum as she nods into her headset. She holds up her finger to me, turns to retrieve my tea, hands it to me just as a big pink bubble bursts flat against her mouth. She moves her mouthpiece to the side.

"Two dollars, fifty cents," she says through sticky lips.

I hand over the exact change, thank her.

The tea is far too sweet, but I take small swallows anyway as I turn around and meander south to the Deming Library. Though inland, east, and still a distance from the glacier-covered peaks of

Mount Baker, Deming has the feel of a mountain town. Ski shops, and pie and coffee houses dot the highway, along with signs warning of last stops for fuel. In between thick forests of trees, I occasionally spot the chimneys of log houses or cabins, smoke swirling and dissipating into the air. Out here, I pretend I've traveled a long way from home. I'm a brave, bold woman. My own woman. Not a wife or daughter, not a victim or a troublemaker, just me.

I swing into the Deming Library parking lot and back up to the door. A younger woman, around my age, is waiting to help unload the van. We smile, greet each other as we move boxes. I don't know her, and she doesn't know me. I consider playing out my daydream and introducing myself to her as someone I am not, but instead I remain quiet. It's better I revel privately in my thoughts. I climb into the van and head back to Central Services.

All too soon for me, a permanent driver is found. I'll return to my regular duties and the new "Jason," who is female and rumored to be gay, will take over.

two

The only gay person I've ever known is my cousin-by-marriage, Tommy. When he was fourteen and I was twelve, his dad married my first cousin. I liked him right away. He was polite, nice to me, and Mom said he was a good Christian boy. We ran into each other over the years at family reunions and picnics and then, in 1990, the year I married Chet, I learned via the family grapevine that Tommy was gay. I was stunned, but his parents—especially his father—were outraged. There was a falling-out of which I heard varying versions, and in the end, Tommy moved to San Francisco. He may as well have dropped smack into the heart of Sodom and Gomorrah for how everyone fretted over his soul and prayed for his salvation.

Two years later, being gay isn't anywhere nearer to being accepted by my family, the community I live in, or by me. I'm acutely aware of the God-forbidden immorality of homosexuality. I easily recall specific verses to support my belief. Verses like

Leviticus 18:22: "Thou shalt not lie with mankind, as with womankind: it is an abomination." Or Leviticus 20:13: "If a man also lies with mankind, as he lieth with a woman, both of them have committed an abomination: they shall surely be put to death." Or one I learned as a God-fearing young teen, Revelation 21:8: "But as for the cowardly, the faithless, the detestable, as for murderers, the sexually immoral, sorcerers, idolaters, and all liars, their portion will be in the lake that burns with fire and sulfur, which is the second death." I'm likewise aware of the stigma borne by being gay. Gays are responsible for AIDS. Gays lure troubled youth into their dark, perverse way of living. Gays are a threat to traditional family values. Or, so I'm ruminating as I peer over the stacks to get a better look at the new hire. I check out her spiky coffee-and-cream-colored hair, her khaki shorts, and unlaced, gray high tops. She isn't fat exactly, but rather solid, sturdy, maybe somewhat masculine—the way I imagine lesbians look. But when she turns to the side and I catch a look at her profile, the way she fills out her T-shirt, there's no mistaking she's female. She spins her head in my direction and I duck out of view. A few minutes later, she rounds the stacks with my manager.

"Lorinda, this is Robin."

Robin thrusts out her hand and squeezes mine.

"Howdy." Her lips turn up into a half-smile.

We stand so close, I can smell her spearmint chewing gum, count the number of freckles dotting her nose. Suddenly, I feel dizzy. My mouth is moving in reply, but my words are drowned by the deafening sound of fireworks exploding in my ears. Robin continues to smile, continues to hold my hand. If I were the slightest bit self-aware, I'd recognize love at first sight. But in this moment, all I know for sure is how at home my hand feels in hers, that I want to be much closer to her, to be enveloped by her. Then the manager is escorting her away to meet the other employees and the spell is broken.

Once Robin begins her new position in earnest, taking over Jason's duties as the main delivery driver, to my relief, the staff speaks less frequently of him and I finally feel permitted to move on. Working with Robin is easy. She treats me respectfully. She doesn't bark orders at me but rather requests my help, even though helping her is part of my job. By the time I show up to the library each morning, she has the delivery van pulled into the garage and is humming and busily arranging boxes in the back. A cup of coffee, steam swirling and dissipating into the air, habitually sits close by. She describes herself as a happy human and I have to agree. She hums or sings quietly to herself and often breaks into what I refer to as her "happy dance."

When Robin asks about my husband during one of our longer delivery rides together, I don't want to answer. Not because I don't trust her, but because I fear speaking of Chet will break the magic I feel in her presence. But she continues probing and eventually, I cave. I've recited the story of my child-bride marriage so many times the words flow like a well-rehearsed script.

"Chet asked me to marry him when I was sixteen while we watched a movie across the street from the drive-in, because we couldn't afford the price of admission."

Robin's eyebrows rise in question and her mouth lifts into an amused half-smile.

"Later, he sold his motorcycle to buy me a ruby ring and we were married ten days after I graduated high school. We bought a house three months later."

She slows the van at a four-way stop. She turns to look at me, and I feel a rush of warmth through my body.

"Chet wants to have babies now," I continue, "but I want to wait, because I don't feel ready."

She reaches over, gives my hand a squeeze. Her simple gesture makes me feel seen and genuinely heard. I'm buffered by my positive experience, so I ask her if she lives with anyone. But all she offers up is that she resides with her roommate, Lauren, in an apartment they rent. She doesn't elaborate on their relationship and in fact, quits talking all together. I try not to feel hurt, but I don't prod, either. I turn my gaze to the wheat fields whipping by my window. I've never had a lesbian friend before and I don't know what religious ramifications, if any, there will be in having one. But if I don't know for certain she is a lesbian, then I don't have to contemplate, and, more importantly, I don't have to shut down the unfolding I'm experiencing in her presence.

In 1994, Robin and I have been working together two years. My world is small, and my peer circle is even smaller. At twenty-two years old, I've been married four years. I rarely see my friends from high school—they've pretty much moved on with their lives. Most are finishing up college, and my best friend, Aimee, is in a serious relationship with a guy her grandma wants her to marry, which means we hardly see each other.

Robin and I work together forty hours a week, primarily alone, in the shipping room or out on deliveries. We occupy a significant amount of time in each other's lives and I'm enthralled with her. She's only five years older, but she knows things I don't and has had experiences I haven't—she's lived much more than I have. Under her worldly influence, I've even branched out from listening solely to contemporary Christian radio stations to listening to a local pop station as well. I quickly discover that pop radio arms me with a plethora of arbitrary information I don't even know I've been missing. This is the case on May 6, 1994, when I learn on my way to work that Lisa Marie Presley has married Michael Jackson. I'm literally vibrating with excited anticipation to share the news with Robin.

I pull into the parking lot, snag my lunch, and bounce into the shipping room. I'm practically exploding with my astonishing news of Lisa Marie and MJ, hoping Robin hasn't already heard. But I burst through the door to discover Robin wiping tears from her eyes. I freeze, I've never seen her cry. Suddenly, I'm unsure how to proceed. Finally, I wrap my arms awkwardly around her.

"What's wrong?"

"Ah, nothin' darlin'." She untangles from me and the bright smile I'm accustomed to spreads across her face. Clearly, she's upset about something. I want her to trust me.

"You can tell me," I say, as I touch her shoulder.

"I'm fine." She shrugs my hand away.

I suck in my breath; I'm startled by her response. Without looking at me or saying another word, Robin grabs her jacket in one hand, her coffee in the other, and walks out the door. Of course, today would be the day she traveled alone to the smaller branches. I get a sinking feeling in my gut, fire behind my eyes. I pinch my nose to keep from crying. There's no denying I feel hurt she hasn't confided in me, but even more, I feel wounded by her rejection.

I drape my jacket over the back of my chair and pick up my lunch. I wander into the main part of the library, down the hall to the staff room. The room is empty, aside from Hope, one of the department managers. Since her recent divorce, she is donning a brand-new look. Her traditional clothing has been replaced with form-fitting, stylish outfits. She's also dyed her hair crimson, cut it into a spike, and pierced her nose and her eyebrow. And her tattoos are increasing. Beginning as tiny flower buds on her ankles, they've spread quickly up her calves and sprouted out her shirt sleeves before wrapping in vines around her fingers. Her normally light skin now takes on spectacular floral hues. Our conservative coworkers express their shock at her transformation behind her back. And even though I also consider myself to be conservative, I secretly admire Hope for her fearlessness. She and I aren't close friends, but we're pleasant to each other. This morning, however, she visibly avoids me by putting on her headphones. If my mind wasn't already preoccupied with Robin, I might take more notice of Hope. Instead, I shove my lunch into the fridge and walk back to the shipping room without a thought.

Two librarians bent head-to-head in the shipping room are whispering when I enter. I can't help but hear one of them asking, "You're sure Hope is having an affair with Robin's partner?"

I stop in my tracks, my mouth surely hanging open. Noticing me, they quit talking, hand me the books in their arms. They instruct me as to which branches they want them sent to, but I hear nothing beyond the word *partner.* As innocent as I may be in the ways of the world, I know having an affair with somebody's partner makes that partner more than a platonic roommate. So, Robin had kept this intimate part of her life from me. I falsely believed we were closer than we are. But simultaneously, I'm struck with another thought. Robin *was* in a relationship with Lauren and now that she *isn't,* she is free.

I shake my head, allow the somber reality of the situation to settle on my heart. Now that I know—really know—I have a responsibility as a Christian to tell Robin the truth about homosexuality. But I don't want to push her away, either; I can't bear to lose her. I have no capacity for imagining my days without her. I haul the stack of books from the librarians to my desk. I pack and secure the box with packing tape, reach for a label; I can't remember where I'm to send them.

I'm still deep in thought and have accomplished little by the time Robin returns. She chucks the van keys on her desk.

"Ready?" She bears no resemblance to the woman she was a few hours earlier. It's clear she has no intention of revisiting the incident.

Our daily routine, once she returns from her solo deliveries, is to go for a walk at the soccer fields. We have a fifteen-minute break, and, when the weather cooperates, being outside is a welcome change. We stand along the curb waiting to cross and I can't keep my eyes from turning toward her. I know I'm staring, but I can't stop myself.

"Hey darlin'," Robin chuckles, "not that I mind being checked out, but are you looking for something in particular?"

A car sails by and Robin yanks me onto the road. We sprint across the street. At the field, we fall into a relaxed pace, but I'm at a loss for conversation. We walk in silence for a few minutes.

I hear Robin exhale slowly. "You heard what happened?"

I shrug, continue to look at the ground.

"Look, I don't want to make a big deal out of it," she says. "I mean Lauren and I were pretty much over. I just didn't realize she was leaving me for Hope."

But I'm still digesting the part where she and Lauren were a couple, and now they weren't because of Hope. "So, you're uh, I mean you are a . . ."

Robin stops walking. For a minute, she appears puzzled. Then, realization begins to settle in, and her voice becomes pinched. "I'm what?" she insists. "What, Lorinda? I'm what?"

My throat constricts; she's never been angry with me before.

"Does it make a difference?"

I don't want it to, but I know it does. I'm unable to recognize any relationship outside of the godly, heterosexual model I've been brought up to believe in. I have no place for sympathy for the loss of Lauren in Robin's life. I feel only my loss at finding out my friend is on the wrong side of God.

"No," I reply, then quickly add, "but if you give yourself to God, your feelings for women will go away and you'll no longer be tempted."

Robin shoves her hands in her short's pockets.

"Well thank you, Pastor Lorinda. Shit, why didn't I think of that?" She steps away from me and her jaw is set.

"Look," she snaps, "I'm gay and I'm fine with it. I thought you were, too. I guess I was wrong."

"You probably just need to meet the right man." I slap my hand over my mouth, blink back the sting of tears.

"Like *you* did?" Robin hisses.

I feel the color draining from my face. The tiniest glint of anger flares inside as I take offense instead of responsibility for being the original offender.

"I happen to love Chet," I retort through pursed lips. "And I'm happy." I flee, darting across the street back to the library.

If I could be honest, I'd admit that even before Robin came into my life, I had difficulty accepting the Holy Bible and my church leaders at face value. I never voiced these doubts aloud. Instead, on the surface, I appear stoic in my faith. I've been taught that God's greater purpose may not be obvious to me, but as a Christian, I'm to follow. But never has my faith caused me to question a relationship with someone so valuable to me. My friendship with Robin has been practically perfect until now. Yet, I can't deny that the Bible, my church, and even my family agree homosexuality is an abomination. Further conflicting is how closely Robin's values seem to align with mine. She treasures her family, is kind, compassionate, and a dedicated employee. I've even heard her speak of her belief in God. She doesn't seem a threat to my morality in any way except for being gay. And I have never even considered that a person's sexual orientation may not be a choice but rather simply who God made them to be. On top of acknowledging she's gay, Robin's insinuation that Chet and I aren't meant for each other churns in my brain.

The next couple of days I give Robin the cold shoulder and she returns the gesture. The uneasiness between us grows and secretly I long to end the silence, but I'm too confused, too unsure of myself to make the first move. So, when a week after our quarrel Robin flops into her rolling chair and wheels herself directly into me, my heart flutters with hope. I pretend her chair isn't pressed up next to my leg, even as she remains and flips coolly through the pages of an oversized book.

"Hey darlin'." She closes the book. "How about we call a truce on this silent treatment?"

I shrug.

She rolls her chair back, clasps her hands in front of her, prayer-like. "I apologize. Okay?"

My tears come too quickly. I look away, embarrassed.

"Hey." She rolls back to my desk. "I really *am* sorry. I shouldn't have said what I did. I didn't mean it."

I swipe at my face. "I'm fine," I choke.

Robin stands and wraps her arms around me. Instantly, I feel relief flooding throughout my entire body. I lean into her. I need her strength and support in my life because the truth is, I'm *not* fine and what I can't yet accept or articulate is that Robin is right, and my relationship with Chet is not fine, either.

three

Whenever I ask Chet where he sees himself in five, ten, or fifteen years, he replies with the same answer. "With you, baby." He holds my head firmly between his hands and says, "All I've ever wanted is to be married and have kids."

Chet and I had sex before we married, only with each other, but it was why I had said yes when he'd proposed. To marry anyone else would have been considered adultery, and I didn't want to compound my sins. Our lovemaking was not particularly enjoyable for me, but I felt I owed him—he was my husband, after all. I'd hoped becoming his wife would create for me an effortless and starry-eyed sexual desire for him. But as soon as our wedding night arrived, I realized the feelings I had even for marital sex were anything but passionate. Chet pushed for sex daily, insisting I should be flattered by how much he wanted me, but I wasn't. I felt repulsed, suffocating with anxiety. I couldn't decipher sexual touch as anything other than negative, shameful, and wrong. My mind fought to separate what was happening with Chet from what had happened with my uncle, or men like Jason, but my heart wouldn't allow it. I feigned illness, said I was too tired, and, of course, used excuses like PMS and my period to the max. But when I complained that having intercourse hurt, that's when Chet put his foot down. He didn't believe me, and so he took me to the doctor in search of answers.

Because he is my husband, I don't feel I have the right to refuse his presence during my examination. He sits near my head in the chair provided to him, mouth set in a line, but his blue eyes glass as if he is about to cry, looking every bit the troubled and affectionate husband. I don't doubt he is concerned, but I know Chet is also there to make a point, to prove that his reality trumps mine.

I scoot my butt to the edge of the exam table, settle my feet into the familiar stirrups. Normally, this is where I float off in my mind, count in my head as if there's not a man's head between my knees probing with metal tools at the most private and sensitive parts of my body. But with Chet holding my hand, I find it impossible to leave and remain uncomfortably grounded in the present. The doctor unscrews and removes the clamp and I feel my muscles relax. He puts the stirrups down, helps me to a sitting position. I pull the far-too-thin paper drape tighter around my breasts and legs, hear it rip up the side.

"Well, I'll send this in, but everything appears normal." The doctor places the swab in a vial. "Maybe your problems are psychological and manifesting as physical," he suggests, without a hint of warmth.

Chet exhales, as if he's been holding his breath the entire time. The doctor's proclamation seems to vindicate his belief that he's doing nothing wrong; the problem lies with me. The doctor pats my back and suggests Chet and I use lubricating cream when engaging in intercourse. I feel my face flushing with humiliation. I knew the doctor wouldn't find a medical reason for my pain, but I had hoped he would. Now I put my feelings aside just the same; they don't matter anyway.

I remind myself that Chet is my husband and that a healthy, godly sexual relationship with him is not only a command, but a gift from God. But what I have no way of knowing is that over time, as our love-making becomes more aggressive, more demanding on his end, it can no longer be deemed healthy. I've never been taught to view my body as mine. I don't believe I have the right to say no to being touched, even by my husband. Obviously, Chet doesn't know either, as he often whispers in my ear, "You know you're mine." I assure myself he only means his words to convey his devotion to me. He doesn't mean to be controlling or possessive. I have to tell myself these things because I can't yet accept the hidden kernel of truth buried deep in my heart—that maybe I don't want to be married to Chet at all.

In late August 1994, whether by the divine hand of God or a missed birth control pill, I discover I'm pregnant. Chet's elated. He's wanted a baby since we married, but I've managed to put him off. Having been raised around many cousins—fifty-six first cousins on my dad's side, alone—I've seen childcare up close. I've observed firsthand the tension babies put on couples, and I fear I'll have a baby, only to wish I hadn't.

Then, there's Robin. We've reached a spot in our relationship where we've agreed to disagree. I even joke with her that I'll make her a Christian before she makes me gay. She chuckles, rolls her eyes, tells me we can't make anyone anything. But I make her conversion my mission. Being pregnant changes everything. When I have the baby, I'll be on maternity leave for three months, and even when I return, it won't be full-time. Chet and I agree we don't want a daycare raising our kids, so I will drop down to part-time. Robin seems happy about my pregnancy, but secretly I hope she will miss me as much as I know I'll miss her.

Chet becomes increasingly invested in the health of my pregnancy. He badgers me less frequently about sex. The reprieve doesn't last long enough, though, because our son, Michael, arrives seven weeks prematurely. Weighing in at five pounds and two ounces, his skin is so translucent I can see his blood pulsing through his veins. He doesn't have eyebrows, eyelashes, or even fingernails. Within the protective walls of the incubator, his tiny chest rises and falls, and I know I'll never feel about anyone else the way I feel about him. I'm overcome with an intense urgency to shield him and to guarantee his safety and happiness. My family doctor and the obstetrician who delivers Michael assure me he's progressing well. He's gaining weight and will be released to go home soon. Still, I can't stave off the worry, and the worry brings on darkness.

As far back as I can remember, despondency has been like a security blanket I've grown accustomed to snuggling. When life becomes more than I can cope with, I find it easier to slink away from the sun, to hide in the shadows. I also discover the best way to keep order in my mind is to keep myself in motion. This isn't difficult, since once we're home, Michael's demands are infinite. From breastfeeding, to constantly holding and rocking him, my body belongs less to me now than before I was pregnant. When he's finally asleep, instead of sleeping myself, I scrub floors, walls, and cupboards. While he lounges in his swing, I vacuum rugs, wash and fold laundry. Dinner is made and on the table before Chet returns home from work each night. Even if Michael is fussy, my nerves are frayed, and fantasies of running away infiltrate my mind, I assure my baby is fed and awaiting his father.

For Chet, Michael is more an elaborate accessory, an adorable, mini version of himself to dress up and show off in public. But Chet works all day and plays softball most nights, so the bulk of Michael's care is left to me, and I'm absolutely worn out. My parents and Chet's parents are in their forties and work full-time, and even though both sets of grandparents enjoy watching Michael, their availability is limited. I'm not particularly close to the women in my church, and being married young and now having a kid has naturally distanced me from my peers, who remain mostly unmarried. Even my best friend, Aimee, and I have drifted at this point in our lives, and we've been friends since kindergarten. She's in love with a guy who lives at least an hour south of us and I'm completely immersed in caring for Michael. We're in completely different stages of life right now, which is hard. I feel as if even my friendship with Robin is on pause. Not that I don't want to call her or see her. I think about her daily, but I can't bring myself to dial her number. The thing is, I want our friendship to remain as it was. What if merging the mothering part of my life with our work relationship changes us? I can't explain why, but I'm afraid she'll treat me differently.

Then, a month into my maternity leave, Robin visits. She strides into my living room, enveloping me in a bear hug. I feel myself relax in her embrace. I inhale her scent, lose myself in the warmth of her familiarity. I let myself slow down in a way I haven't been able to since I brought my baby home. Robin pulls away and her eyes search the room for Michael. I point to the swing where he's fallen asleep. She nods and we sit together on the couch. I can feel heat, see light radiating from her, pulling me from my tunnel of darkness. I fight the urge to hug her again. She drops a gift into my lap.

"Oh," I say with surprise. I hadn't noticed her bringing anything in with her. "Should I open it?"

"Yeah," Robin chuckles, and I slip my fingers under the tape.

I meticulously remove the paper, fold it in half, then lift off the box lid. Inside is a handmade quilt with Michael's name and the date of his birth embroidered along one edge.

"This is mine!" Robin elbows me playfully in the arm and points to a green fish swimming in a blue square, a nod to a joke we shared about the amount of tuna fish I eat.

"I get it." I nudge her back.

Then I tear up as I realize the quilt is made up of many squares individually crafted by my coworkers. I inspect each block of the quilt, identifying the creators by their initials embroidered in the corner of their patch. Robin catches me up on the library happenings. I imagine the faces of each person she speaks of and I feel more connected to my life. This heartfelt gift lifts my spirits enough to remind me there's a world outside of my four walls.

"Work is not nearly as fun without you, though."

"Yeah, right." I roll my eyes. "You probably haven't even noticed I'm gone."

"No, really." She meets my gaze and I see her expression is serious.

The intensity of her attention makes me look away, but I feel my breath quickening. She misses me. I have a sudden urge to throw my arms around her, yelling "take me with you!" Michael begins to fuss, and I feel my nipples sting as the milk drips down to my stomach. I stand and fold my arms over my chest.

"I really should get going." Robin stands to go.

Without unfurling my arms, I lean in and we embrace awkwardly.

"I—" I start, but I can't come up with the right words. There are so many things I want to say to her. I watch as she walks down the steps, gets in her car, and drives away.

four

I return to the library when Michael is three months old. My emotions are a whirlwind of contradictions. As much as I long to reenter the real world, leaving my infant causes my heart to ache. Not that I can stay home full-time anyway; I can't. Even though Chet makes a decent amount of money, he also spends a considerable amount. When I freak out about the amount of money he's blowing through, he buys something for me, and then I feel like I can't complain.

On the drive from the sitter's place to the library, my hands shake on the steering wheel. I park next to Jo's car and walk around to the back of the library. In the distribution room, Robin works at her desk packing a box, her back to me. Without hesitation, I throw my arms around her from behind.

She turns around, smiles. "Well, howdy, darlin'."

"I missed you so much." I squeeze her tight.

Returning to the library is exactly the mental stimulation I need. But caring for a baby demands continuous amounts of energy, and I find myself physically depleted. Moving from under the wings of my parents directly to my husband has done little to prepare me for the realities of adulthood. I often feel as if I'm playing house—cooking, cleaning, and rearing a child, just as my mother did. Sometimes when Chet is away and Michael is quietly napping in his room, I stare into my bedroom mirror and wonder what my life could have been like if Chet and I had never married, if I'd never had a baby. Frequently, my thoughts settle on Robin—her crooked half-smile, her easy laugh—and I wish I still worked with her full-time. As much as I want to be with Michael, I also desire to be with Robin.

Then, one afternoon as we pack boxes, Robin casually suggests coming to my house to hang out after work. I feel my skin throb, I resist the urge to scream *Yes!* Instead, I shrug as if I'm fine either way. Robin shrugs back, closes the box she's filled.

"Okay. If you don't want me to, that's cool."

"I want you to!" I answer too quickly, with too much enthusiasm. "Maybe tomorrow. Let me ask Chet."

Chet subscribes wholeheartedly to his jealous idea that all men are out to steal me away from him, and now I wonder if he'll feel the same about Robin. He knows from conversations between Jo and me that Robin is gay. Even though I dream about her when we aren't together, I haven't asked myself what that might mean about my relationship with Chet or what it means about me. So, the following morning as we are getting ready for work, I summon up my courage to approach Chet.

"So, I'm wondering if it'd be cool if Robin hung out after work at our house?" I glance at his face.

"I have softball tonight. Doubleheader." He pulls his jacket over his work shirt.

I'm not sure if that's his answer or if he's saying I shouldn't have her over while he's away. I loop my arm under Michael's car seat handle and scoop up the diaper bag with my free hand. Once we're both on the front porch, Chet locks the door behind us, then takes Michael's car seat from me. He buckles Michael into my car and gives us each a peck on the cheek. Before heading to his car, he grasps my arm, pulls me into him.

"I guess she can," he says, "but don't let her take you away from me." Then he rubs his nose against mine and laughs.

But I walk away feeling a tinge of concern I can't explain.

I don't want to appear overly eager, so I refrain from rushing directly to Robin's desk when I get to work. By lunchtime, I can no longer contain myself.

"Hey," I say, a little more high-pitched than I'd intended.

"What's up?" Robin retrieves her coffee and an apple from her desk.

"I'm wondering if you're busy after work?" I pull a tuna sandwich from my bag.

"Yeah, super busy." She shakes her head in contradiction.

"Well, then . . ." I can't keep a smile from spreading across my face. "You want to come over?"

Robin tilts her head to the side, takes a bite of her apple. "Sure, little lady. Sounds fun."

That night, all through dinner, as I clear the dinner dishes, and even after I've shuffled Chet out the door to his softball game, I eagerly anticipate Robin's arrival. I rock Michael to sleep and lay him carefully in his crib. I fluff up the cushions on the couch and straighten the magazines on the coffee table. I shake out my hair and apply, then reapply, my lip gloss. I check the time: seven-thirty. Chet will be through his first game. Maybe Robin's changed her mind about coming over. We didn't set a specific time. I told her any time after dinner was fine. I plop down on the couch, exhale, slow my breath. *What's going on, why do I care so much?* Just act normal, be normal. A knock on the front door brings me back, and I shoot off the couch. I push open the door. Robin balances an oversized can of tuna on her hip, grins.

"Howdy, darlin'. A gift for the hostess."

I laugh, invite her in.

After her first visit, I'm less timid about asking Chet if she can come by. He willingly grants his approval and even begins playing pick-up for other softball teams. But I no longer care how often or how long he's gone, because with the promise of Robin's company, all else fades into the background. Before long, she's coming by most nights of the week. Our time together is casual, easy. She gets down on the floor and plays with Michael while I wash dishes or fold laundry and we chat. Once Michael is down for the night, we flop down on the couch, her at one end, me at the other. But even despite our purposeful physical distance, the pull between us is undeniable. In those moments alone with Robin, something inside of me begins to further unfurl and I crave more.

One night, instead of retreating to my end of the sofa, I boldly stretch out horizontally and rest my feet in Robin's lap. She smiles, wraps her hands around my feet, and begins to rub and knead at my soles. Slowly, she moves up my ankles to the tight muscles of my calves and I feel my body melt into the couch cushions. Gently, she tugs at my legs, pulls my body closer to hers, and I stiffen. In response, Robin's hands grow still, and she slides them back to my feet, where she squeezes to conclude the massage before pulling her hands away. I sit up and her eyes catch mine, and for a second, we hold each other's gaze. The whole thing is almost imperceptible. She can pretend nothing's happened if I don't challenge her. I can pretend, too, if she doesn't say anything that will confuse me.

"Your muscles are tight!" she laughs, breaking the spell.

"Yeah." I swing my legs off the couch and stand.

Robin stands, too. "I should probably get going." She puts on her jacket.

I walk her to the door, give her a quick hug, and she's gone. But the memory of her touch lingers. As someone who's made a habit of living outside of her own body, the exhilaration I feel as I imagine her hands rubbing against my skin confuses me. What I do know is I'm meant to be Chet's wife. Jesus says that if anyone wants to follow him, they must deny themselves and carry their own cross. Therefore, there would be no point in asking myself what's going on with my feelings for Robin.

five

Robin loves camping and hiking. And bugs. And dirt. She views camping as a vacation. I do not. I enjoyed camping with my family as a child, but we camped in a motorhome, not on the ground. We belonged to a camping resort with a pool and a store. So, when Robin suggests I go along with her one weekend, I quickly remind her I'm not a nature person. Besides, how can I leave home for an entire weekend? I've never left Michael, now eighteen months old, overnight—even with Chet.

"Come on," Robin coaxes, "you deserve a break, a real break."

I try to imagine my body without Michael hanging from my hip.

"Lorinda, moms leave for a couple of days at a time. He does have a father."

I feel torn. I'm so very tired of working myself to the bone to keep thoughts of unworthiness from floating into my consciousness, working to find ways of avoiding Chet's groping, to find other ways of pleasing him that might make up for my failures. Robin's enthusiasm doesn't wane, neither does her insistence that I'm owed a well-deserved rest. And even though we haven't shared another moment like we had that evening on the couch, I continue to crave her attention. Eventually, I cave and tell Chet about Robin's offer. I don't expect him to tell me flat out I can't go, but I decide if I detect the slightest hint he doesn't want me to go, I'll give up the idea.

"You should definitely go. Have some fun!" he responds.

I'm wary of Chet's good-natured agreement to my absence.

"You're sure?" I search his eyes in case I'm missing something.

"Yep! Me and the big guy will be fine, won't we?" He plants a kiss on Michael's nearly bald head.

"What will you do without me?" I feel panicky as I realize Chet is not going to be my out.

"Watch television, eat junk food, all the stuff we can't do when you're here." He winks playfully.

Well crap. I have his blessing and no legitimate excuse not to go. Except maybe one, I'll be alone overnight with Robin. I feel my heart beat faster at the thought.

"I think Fort Ebey is about sixty miles away," Robin announces, signaling it's time to get going. "I'm definitely going to need an espresso."

We climb into her "vintage" car, as she refers to it. The front seat is one especially long, tattered bench seat, and it's sticky.

"Just a little spilled Mountain Dew," Robin clarifies as she pokes at foam sticking up through the ripped vinyl.

She starts the engine, pushes in a protruding cassette tape, and Tracy Chapman's "Give Me One Reason" fills the car. Robin sings along, tossing her head back, swaying side to side. At the espresso stand she hand-cranks the car window open, it gets stuck three-quarters of the way down. She sticks her head out the window, unfazed, and cheerfully orders two espresso drinks from the barista.

"Oh, I don't care for coffee." I hold up my hand.

"Well then, darlin', maybe you haven't met the right coffee," Robin says with a wink.

She means to be funny, but I can't help but wince. The espresso machine whirs, and a barista flies around measuring and pouring. The rich aroma of roasted coffee beans brings back memories of my dad. He had coffee every morning, and its fragrance lingered in the house long after he'd pulled out of the driveway and headed off to work.

Robin hands me the steaming paper cup. I sip at the frothy, milky liquid and feel its warmth spread throughout my chest. I give Robin a nod of approval and she smiles knowingly.

By the time we reach our destination, I've waffled a million times between whether I should have or should not have agreed to this camping excursion. Finally, I must admit I'm too far away to do anything but try to relax. Robin is a camping ace and has the car unpacked and the tent up promptly. Trying to be helpful, I pull our sleeping bags from the back of the car, but Robin grabs them from me and points me in the direction of a camp chair she's set up.

"Sit," she instructs.

"I can help." But I've already settled in and closed my eyes.

The sun warms my face, waves crash in the distance, and when Robin gently shakes my arm, I realize I've fallen asleep.

"I made something to eat." Robin points a roasting stick with a perfectly cooked wiener in my face.

I'm not overly fond of hot dogs. I haven't had one in years. Of course, I don't want to do anything to hurt her feelings.

Robin waves the stick under my nose. "What are you waiting for?"

I pull it off the stick and toss it back and forth in my hands while it cools. Robin chomps enthusiastically while I take smaller, less ambitious bites.

When the darkness begins to settle around us, blurring our features, Robin puts another log on the fire.

"How does it feel to be free?" she asks, poking at the log with the tip of her roasting stick.

The fire surges, sending a burst of heat and smoke in my direction. I close my eyes.

Free . . . I keep a clean house and a clean baby. I strive to obey God, my parents, and Chet. I live as organized a life as possible. But freedom . . . I open my eyes. Robin is watching me.

"I don't think I know," I confess.

She props her stick against the picnic table and sits down in a chair next to me.

"Darlin'," she sighs softly, "everyone has a right to be free."

I stare into the flames, feel the warmth of my flushing face. But do I? If my primary purpose in life is to live as a disciple of Christ, then freedom only allows me to exist in a world within the bounds of my Christian faith. So how free am I really in comparison to the freedom Robin feels? Sensing my darkening mood, Robin kicks playfully at my heel with her foot. I kick back at her.

"Want to play rummy?" She pushes her chair back, returns with a deck of cards. She takes a seat at the picnic table and shuffles the cards. I sit down across from her.

"You know," she says, "I spent time split between both my parents' houses. My father remarried and my stepmom didn't like my brother and me." She lays a suit of aces on the table.

"What didn't she like about you?"

"I wanted to be a part of my dad's life and she wanted him to herself."

I sense the hurt in her voice. I appreciate that Robin feels close enough to me to share such personal information, but I don't know what to do with it. My fingers press against the cards in my hands, creasing them slightly. I suddenly feel awkward, like I'm spying on a conversation I shouldn't be listening to.

"I'm sorry."

"It's not your fault, darlin'."

I relax a bit. She lays down four eights, then discards a jack of spades to end her turn.

"Did you still see your dad?" I ask. "After he married her?"

"Not much. He chose her over me and my brother."

I feel the weight of what she's sharing in the pit of my stomach and I long to tell her that I'd have chosen her. She motions for me to take my turn, and I draw from the pile. I still have nothing to lay down. She's kicking my butt.

"But my mom married a really nice guy. I call him Papa." She lays down four kings. "So, all good." This is her way, not to wallow in sadness.

We finish the game and Robin snuffs out the waning fire. Fortunately, I'm too tired to dwell on how much I detest sleeping so close to nature. I burrow inside my sleeping bag, leaving only a small gap for air, and drift effortlessly to sleep.

The crackle of burning wood and the smell of frying eggs is enough to rouse me the next morning. I stretch, feeling the achy muscles that come with sleeping on the ground all night. I peer through an opening in my sleeping bag. The tent flap is pulled back enough to let me see Robin perched over the firepit with a frying pan. I stick my head out.

"Howdy, darlin'. How did you sleep?" Robin asks.

I give her two thumbs up. The sun pokes through white clouds and it's chilly but dry. I'm relieved at the sight of eggs, which I enjoy eating.

After breakfast, I pull on an extra jacket and follow Robin to a mountain trail she's anxious to introduce me to. While we hike, our conversation is casual, lighthearted. We discuss music, Robin sings random bits of songs she knows. We summarize books we've read, we joke, we laugh. Occasionally, she points to a plant or, much to my dismay, an insect, and tells me all she knows about it. She truly loves the outdoors in a way I've not learned to. As the trail becomes more rugged, I get quiet, I'm tiring a bit. Robin looks back, her face glowing with perspiration. She keeps moving, but never pulls too far ahead. I try to imagine being on the same hike with Chet. He wouldn't amble. He'd likely try to race to the top of the mountain just to prove his ability to out-climb me. I wonder what Lauren was like with Robin. For the first time since they'd split, I wonder if Robin misses her, what life is like as a single woman.

"Do you think you'll ever get married?" I ask aloud what I'm thinking in my head, then instantly regret it.

To my surprise, she answers. "I'd like to."

"I thought you were gay?" I blurt out.

"You mean to a man?"

"I guess." I'm flustered, not certain what I meant.

"You know I'm gay." I hear a shift in her tone; I've offended her.

Of course, she wouldn't marry a man, but still, I continue to puzzle it out as she leads us farther up the mountain. *So, she'll be alone.*

"But I might meet the right woman," Robin adds softly, just loud enough for me to hear.

Her words send a tingle through my body, my mind races off in several directions. Two women marrying is unheard of, not even legal. But what if God's plan for mankind could be played out in a same-sex union? In my heart, the idea of God expecting Robin to remain alone forever because she loves women seems cruel. Which is impossible because God is love, therefore, he can't be cruel. I'm so engrossed in the controversy in my head, I miss a step and trip over a root. I fall forward, landing hard into Robin. She turns quickly and halts my fall.

"Whoa, you okay?" She wraps her arms around my shoulders, and for a moment, we're breathing together.

I notice the angle of her jaw, the feathered lines at the corner of her eyes, and the crooked smile, now tentative with worry. I have the strongest urge to press myself into her, to let her hold me, protect me, love me.

In my life I've known two kinds of love: the unconditional love I have for my child and the seemingly conditional love I've received from most everyone else. If I perform the way I'm expected, follow the rules, don't make waves, then I'm lovable, maybe even worthy of praise. But if I dare to veer from the path laid before me, I face rejection. But here, with Robin, all those fears fall away. She pulls me closer. My body trembles, but I don't pull away. Her mouth brushes against my cheek, finds my lips. I close my eyes. My body is weightless as I allow myself to sink into the softness of her kiss. How I've ached for this kind of physical connection, this intimacy I've been unable to name. She pulls away, I open my eyes, she's staring at me as if I'm a wild animal she doesn't want to scare away. I step back, touch my fingers to my lips, and then I remember . . . I remember why this feels so familiar.

In sixth grade, Sarah Summers and I flopped onto my waterbed after school. We let our bare feet hang off the edge of the bed. Sarah rested her head in the crook of my arm as we stared up at the posters of Michael J. Fox and Ralph Macchio taped to the ceiling, above.

"Michael J. Fox is obviously the better kisser," she said, turning toward me.

Her long eyelashes brushed my chin, sending electricity through my body as we floated. "What do you think?" she asked.

But all I could see were her full, glossy red lips. On total impulse, I kissed her. Peppermint gum mixed with watermelon lip balm exploded in my mouth. But she shoved me back, slapped her hand over her lips. Before I could say a word, she bolted over the side of the bed, scooped up her backpack, and ran out the door. I was stunned by what I'd done, then terrified she would tell everyone at school. But nothing happened. Nothing, except we didn't remain friends, and I was too ashamed to approach her again, even to apologize.

"Lorinda, I'm . . ." Robin holds her hand out to me, but I turn and run.

If Robin follows, I can't hear her over the voices in my head condemning me for what I've done. My mind fights to make sense of what my body feels. If Chet finds out, if anyone finds out, oh God . . . I reach our campsite, climb into the tent, and zip myself up in my sleeping bag. I squeeze my eyes shut, press my palms hard against them. There's no possible way I can reconcile what has happened. I burrow deeper into my sleeping bag. I kissed a girl—again. I'm sick to my stomach. Am I a lesbian, too? I can't be, *I can't be*. I have to hide.

I know the real sin isn't that Robin kissed me, but that I wanted her to. I shove the notion from my brain. I want to disappear; I don't know what to do or think. So, I do nothing but lie in my sleeping bag and wait. Wait for Robin to come back.

It feels like she's been gone forever and it's black outside by the time she returns. She lays as far from me as she possibly can within the confines of the tent. She breathes quietly, but I doubt she's asleep. I wish I could reach over, give her a playful shove, just pretend like nothing happened. But I'm not in sixth grade and we both know something has happened.

By the time the sun peeks over the shortest treetops, I wake to find Robin's sleeping bag is already gone. Memories of the day before rush back as painfully as brain freeze. I open the tent flap to see Robin has cleaned up most of our gear and is packing the car. I roll my sleeping bag and dump it into the back of the car. Robin quickly disassembles the tent, and we are on our way. We weave along narrow roads in silence. When we exit the preserve, Robin pushes in the cassette tape and Tracy Chapman belts out "Give Me One Reason," her words imploring me to turn around.

I peek at Robin's face; her blue eyes float above un-spilled tears. I feel a lump forming in my own throat. I turn and look out the window. I watch as the trees whip by in a blur of green and wish I'd never agreed to this camping trip. I wish I'd stayed home where I belong, then none of this would be happening.

Once home, I walk up the stairs to the front door. I'm exhausted. Chet is draped across the couch with a video game controller in his hand. Michael sits in a pile of blocks and toy cars sucking on a piece of Red Vine licorice, his mouth covered in bright red stickiness.

"Hey," I drop my bag on the floor.

Michael looks up, smiles. He pulls the licorice through his teeth and holds it out to me.

"Hey hon'." Chet's eyes remain fixed on the television screen. "How did it go?"

"Okay." I go to Michael and kneel in front of him. He wraps his sticky arms around my neck. I hug him close and feel myself tear up. A pang of guilt rips through my heart.

"I think Robin likes me." I blurt, and Chet pauses his game.

"What do you mean 'likes you'?" His eyes bore into mine.

I swallow, remind myself honesty is the key to a successful marriage and take a deep breath.

"I mean like, *likes* me."

"How do you know?" Chet puts the remote down, moves to where I sit on my knees holding Michael.

Michael begins to wriggle and whine in my arms.

"Did she do something?" His hands are on his hips.

The steel blue of his eyes, the way his biceps flex, evoke a memory from the early days of our marriage.

I worked afternoons and evenings, alone in a chocolate shop. One night, as I sat hunched over a book, I heard the door swing open and one of the security guards for the shopping complex walked in.

"Hey." James nodded his head.

He often came into the store to chat after making a lap or two around the parking lot. I enjoyed visiting with him and never worried our visits were anything but friendly.

"Slow night." James ambled to the counter. "You got caramels?"

I pushed open the glass door, reached in and pulled out a milk-chocolate-covered caramel. James handed me a dollar, and when I reached to take it, his hand closed on mine. We made eye contact for a split second, just long enough for Chet to barge through the door.

"What the fuck, James?" Chet's shoulders puffed like peacock's feathers.

James let my hand drop. I hustled from behind the counter, wedged myself between him and Chet.

"Nothing is going on, Chet," I said, speaking quickly.

James raised his hands in the air and backed away. "Just buying some chocolate, man. That's all." Then he winked at me and pushed past Chet.

Chet didn't go after him, but he did wait at the door, arms crossed over his chest until I closed the shop, then we walked together to the car.

"That fucker needs to stay away from you," he grumbled.

The next afternoon as I settled into my shift, I noticed James peering cautiously through the front window. I motioned for him to come in, but he turned away. I got up, walked around the counter, but before I got the front door open, I saw the bruising on his cheek and the cut above his left eye.

"What happened?" I reached up to touch the black bruise, but he stepped back.

"Your psycho husband came after me last night. Held me down with a gun to my head!"

"Lorinda!" Chet's voice rings out like a gunshot, bringing me back.

I focus on his face.

"Did she do anything?"

I shake my head. "No, nothing."

I put Michael down.

Chet tilts his head, narrows his eyes, an expression I know to be wary of. "Because if she did anything, I want to know."

I continue to shake my head. Of course, this isn't the right way to go, I need to backtrack.

"I'm kidding with you." I flash him my most mischievous smile.

I wrap my arms around him and squeeze. Chet's body tenses but he hugs me back.

"Not funny," he murmurs, before returning to the couch and picking up his game controller.

I grab my bag and take it to our bedroom. I sit on the edge of our bed and cover my face with my hands. Oh my God. I must rein this this in, whatever this is. And I must keep away from Robin, from here on out.

six

At work on Monday, my conversations with Robin are clipped. I go about my job as if she were any other coworker. She does the same, until she backs me into a corner of the shipping room.

"Move," I say.

"Not until you talk to me."

"It's better this way for everyone." I push past her.

"Not for me," she says to my back.

This is the second time our friendship has been tested, but the stakes are much higher this time. Last time we had a falling out I was clear on my intentions and convictions; I knew Robin was wrong. But this time, I'm not sure of anything, except that living without her is like trying to live without air and I am quite sure I am suffocating.

Christian girls are expected to stay sexually pure until marriage, but even at the young age of six, I understood that what had occurred between my uncle and me was sexual, sinful. Even with those vile certainties roiling inside, I sometimes wished to be touched in that way again, and so I gave in to my impulses. By stroking myself in the places my uncle had fondled, I blissfully lost myself. Separating from my body, I felt my mind float away. The escape was real and alluring, but immediately following climax, I was flooded with feelings of self-loathing and shame. Those conflicting desires to be both sinless and gratified bombarded me into pubescence, setting me up for a lifetime of flip-flopping from surrender to temptation, and self-hate in the wake of each surrender. I believed Jesus resided inside my heart, and I knew I couldn't run, couldn't hide from my filth, but inevitably my longing for attention outweighed my pursuit for God's approval.

This push-and-pull of my conscience is tortuous, unrelenting, until one night after putting Michael to bed, I announce to Chet I'm going out to get some fresh air. He's sprawled across the couch, engrossed in a video game. He nods in acknowledgement without breaking eye contact with the television. I pull on my sweatshirt and stride out the door into the humid evening. I stroll down the street; I feel almost giddy.

I should turn around. But the farther I walk, the quicker I move. I ignore the voice in my head, yet oddly, I feel fully in my body. Down the street, around the bend, and over the bridge, I register each stride as my feet strike the ground resolutely. An older, worn-down apartment building comes into view. I know this is where she lives; I just don't know which apartment is hers. I slow down, casting sideways glances through sliding glass doors, hoping no one notices. I spot Robin flung across her bed. The hairs on my arms rise. I run up to the sliding door and rattle it.

She leaps off her bed, grabs a baseball bat seemingly out of nowhere, and throws open the sliding door with such force it bounces back. I hold my forearms over my face, hear the bat hit the ground, feel Robin's arms around me.

"I've been waiting for you," she whispers, leading me to her bed.

In her bed, under the spell of her touch, my marital and religious vows dissipate in the heat of our lovemaking. I never dreamed I could derive such pleasure from another's body. Neither could I have conceived of willingly yielding my body without feeling resentment or obligation. Under Robin's gentle, yet capable, touch, my hunger for her only grows and I will seize every opportunity to be with her, but it will never be enough. I know Chet's acceptance of Robin is key to keeping our love affair a secret—and key to keeping Robin in my life. If Chet blesses our friendship, I expect the rest of our family and friends will, also. As such, my attempt to wholly incorporate Robin into our life and marriage, though not entirely conscious, evolves out of necessity. Robin, being naturally outgoing, treats Chet as a friend, discussing sports, cars, or whatever he wants to talk about. And I don't believe she plans or conspires to fool Chet or to take advantage of his trust. I imagine that, like me, she doesn't consider consequences or outcomes. Rather, she only considers her feelings for me. We have no master plan, no plan B, but the longer we get away with our secret, the more confident we grow.

In early spring, on a Saturday, when Chet is away playing baseball, Robin and I decide to have a yard sale. Mom offers to help. I still remember the wet grass sticking to Mom's sandals as she arranged books on a makeshift table of sawhorses and plywood.

Robin and I sit melded together atop the cement steps. Under the cocoon of our blanket, Robin's knee presses into mine, and her hand closes firmly around my fingers. From the yard, Mom holds a worn, plastic dish rack in one hand, while picking grass from her sandal with the other. I've seen to most of the garage sale preparation before she arrives, but she still finds plenty to keep her busy.

"If we price too high, we'll have to carry all this stuff to Goodwill. What do you girls think?"

Robin lets go of my hand and splays her fingers across my thigh. I suck in my breath, nod in agreement. Robin's hand travels covertly up my skirt. A mischievous smile spreads across her lips. Soundlessly, I will her to stop, but my resolve disappears as quickly as her fingers. As if able to read my thoughts, Mom suddenly looks up from her arranging. She tilts her head, narrows her eyes so slightly in a way that only a daughter would notice. I feel instant shame. But my thighs tighten involuntarily around Robin's wrist as she and Mom discuss pricing half-melted candles and earrings missing their mates.

"One earring is perfect for a nose piercing," Robin suggests.

Mom rolls her eyes, tosses both the earring and candles into the "free box." I exhale silently, relaxing my grip on Robin's wrist. She gradually withdraws her fingers, dragging them across my thigh. A slight breeze carries the scent of freshly brewing coffee from the kitchen and Mom takes this as her cue. She wipes her hands on her pants, maneuvers around us on the steps.

"Lorinda, help me with the coffee." Her tone causes me to immediately kick myself free from the blanket and follow her.

My eyes adjust slowly to the darkness of the house. Mom's cold stare comes into focus, causing my stomach to churn. She looms within an inch of my face, gripping two steaming mugs of coffee.

"I don't know what's going on between you and your *friend,* but it needs to stop. You *know* better." She pushes past me, a bit of coffee sloshes from the mugs, splatters on the floor.

I fetch a towel from the counter and bend to wipe up the droplets, but only manage to add to the mess with the tears that drip from my nose. I dash into the bathroom and lock the door. I splash cold water on my face, my heart bangs against my chest. What if Mom says something? What if she tells Chet? As I concentrate on my reflection in the mirror, I labor through a myriad of possible thoughts Mom might be having. I do know better, better than to be so careless in front of Mom. When I've worked up the courage to leave the bathroom, I find Mom and Robin engaged with yard-sale customers. I sit back down on the steps. Mom has returned to her normal self, our encounter seemingly forgotten or at least shelved for the time being. I've dodged a bullet but have come too close for comfort. I know I need to think more closely about what I'm doing with Robin. Our relationship is dangerous, not to mention immoral, and deep down, I know we are living on borrowed time. This is the hard truth of the matter. I vow to myself to never give Mom reason to be suspicious of Robin and me again, then shove the concern to the back of my mind.

Later that night, after Chet's home from softball and dinner's through, I excuse myself for a walk. I of course run straight to Robin's apartment.

"Hey darlin'," she says, leading me to her bed.

I'm near exploding from sexual tension that's been mounting between us all day. Her skin is refreshingly cool against my heated body. The ceiling fan whirrs above us as she peels my clothes away, my nipples hardening under the breeze. Robin's lips curl into a smile as she lowers her mouth to my breasts. She languishes over my body as if she were encountering me for the first time, savoring my flesh, one kiss, one nibble at a time. As badly as I want her to bring me to climax, I also wish to remain suspended in decadent anticipation. Without warning, I sit straight up, alarming Robin, who stops suddenly.

"You take my place." I move over, motion for her to lie down where I've been.

She tosses me a sideways glance but does as she's told. I tug off her shorts but don't bother with her underwear. I nudge them over with my nose, enough to get my mouth, my tongue inside of her. When she begins to moan, I thrust faster and with more pressure until her legs clamp around my head. Her body shakes as waves of orgasms roll through her body. The taste of her on my lips, her wet heat on my chin pushes me into orgasm, and my cry comes out muffled against her thighs.

Afterward, once we've held each other, laughed, kissed, and laughed some more, we prop ourselves up against the headboard. Robin leans over as if to kiss me again and I teasingly push her away.

"Honestly, you wore me out." I smack her with a magazine I found on the floor.

But her expression is serious. I can feel myself tensing up.

"Be with me," she whispers into my ear.

Before I can respond, she bounds off the bed and disappears into the closet. She emerges with a book, front cover-side-down.

"Before you freak out, just let me talk." She flips the book over and I read the title.

"*From Wedded Wife to Lesbian Life.*" I snort.

"This could work. This book is full of women who made a change from being married to men to being with women."

I can't believe what I'm hearing; she's crazy. "You genuinely think reading a book can miraculously avoid destroying my marriage and devastating my family?" I'm incredulous. "And what about Michael?" I get up, snatch my clothes from the floor.

"I'll take care of you *and* Michael. You know we belong together."

Even as her eyes cloud with tears, I know the opposite is true. We do *not* belong together. In fact, I belong to Chet and even more significantly to God. Why have I let this go on for so long? Being a lesbian is not an option. Not in my family and not in my religion. My family and friends would disown me, Chet would take Michael from me. I reach for the sliding door, but Robin holds it shut.

"How long are you going to do this to us?" Her face is now flush with anger.

"To us?"

"Yes, us! What about me?"

But I don't have an answer.

Addicted to the sexual and emotional void she fills in me, I never think to ask her what she wants or needs from our relationship. I yank her hand from the door, push it open, and take off, running back to where I belong.

seven

Robin ignores me the entire following week at work. I fight the urge to talk to her, though I'm not even sure what I would say. I know she's right. I haven't given a thought to how she feels because I am too preoccupied trying to keep her a secret. I know we aren't supposed to be together, but without her, I feel anxious, untethered, and unable to think clearly. I decide I have to make a move, show her how much she means to me before I lose her altogether.

On Friday, I approach Robin with an apology for running out on her. To my relief, she wraps me in a hug.

I pull back so I can see her face, "Will you come stay the night Saturday?"

"Overnight? Are you sure?"

Well, no, I'm not sure. I'm not sure of anything except that I need her, but I bob my head in confirmation. Chet has a tournament out of town and won't be back until late afternoon Sunday.

Robin whoops aloud, grabs me around the waist, and swings me in a circle.

Saturday morning, Chet bends down, kisses my cheek. He smells of stale sleep. The brim of his baseball hat tousles my hair and I root deeper into the blankets.

"I'll be back Sunday night." He hefts his bat bag over his shoulder and turns to go.

I peer from my cocoon as he pulls his hat down farther over his black hair. I watch his broad shoulders disappear through the door. When I hear his car pull away from the curb, I swing my legs out of bed. From the bottom of a drawer I seldom open, I pull a soft pink camisole nightie. I undress, fold my T-shirt and worn-out long johns, my usual sleeping attire, and lay them in the drawer. The silky fabric of the nightie slips over my body but clings to my breasts and hips. I step in front of the full-length mirror, push down the niggling fear threatening to dampen my anticipation. From the opposite end of our tiny house, I hear a faint tapping on the window. I shove open the bedroom door, creep quietly to Michael's room and peek in on him. The soft hum of his breathing assures me he is sound asleep. I slide across the hardwood floor of the living room directly into the kitchen. I press my nose against the window. Robin peers from the other side, a hint of a smile playing at the corner of her mouth. She's remained hidden alongside the garage, watching for Chet to drive off before sneaking through the fence. I fling open the door and yank her inside. We both giggle. Her eyes widen as she takes in my skimpy negligee. I turn a circle in front of her, flicking my hair dramatically over my shoulder.

"Want coffee?" I ask, giving her a suggestive wink.

Robin shakes her head, wraps her arms around me. "Bedroom" she breathes into my neck.

Barely inside the bedroom door, Robin steps out of her jeans, pulls off her sweatshirt, and tosses it on the floor. She runs her hands up and down over my smooth nightie before finally pulling it over my head. We fall across the bed, still warm from where I burrowed moments earlier. "Marriage should be honored by all, and the marriage bed kept pure, for God will judge the adulterer and all the sexually immoral," the condemning words of Hebrews hiss from deep within my conscience. I tense. But Robin traces my face slowly with her finger and I feel my skin melting.

"I love you." She brushes her lips along my neck, and I lose all inhibition.

Intimacy with her is so intoxicating, the rest of the world, my obligations, the commands of the Bible, I simply disregard them all. My body burns with desire as she peppers my skin with kisses. Slowly, deliberately she travels down my body, her tongue, lips, fingers all expertly finding just the right places and exerting just the right amount of pressure. Not until after I've cried out, sat up, then fallen back dramatically against the pillows, arms spread wide, does Robin crawl up and lie down next to me. She leans over me, a smile playing at her lips as I run my hand through her spikey hair and pull her in for a kiss. My thigh barely grazes the wet spot between her legs and I feel her shudder. I roll her over onto her back, she spreads her legs and I move in between them. She reaches her hand down, grabs my hand, and squeezes as my tongue slips inside of her. I can sense a fire building again inside of me when suddenly I hear a door slam. Robin and I freeze. Who would just walk into my house? Unless . . .

"Lorinda?" I hear Chet's bat bag hit the floor, the aluminum bats clanging together.

Unless Chet hasn't gone anywhere at all. Unless he's been spying the whole time, probably lurking outside the bedroom window. My body is heavy. Chet's footsteps grow louder, the closer he gets to the bedroom. Robin and I don't have more than a few seconds to decide what to do, but somewhere between hearing Chet's voice and moving into defensive action, I'm flooded with emotion. The reality of what's happening is striking me square in the face. My disobedience to God, to Chet, is about to be revealed for the whole world to see. I'm the prostitute Jesus approached at the well; I've sinned, and now I'm going to be exposed. What will my family think? Chet will obviously tell them. And what about Michael? He'll never let me have Michael. Oh my God, oh my God. I search the room frantically for my clothes and find a sweatshirt on the floor—Robin's sweatshirt. I pull it over my head, yank it down to cover my thighs. Robin leaps out of bed and tugs on her jeans.

Chet is at the bedroom door now and there's nowhere to escape to, no alternative exit, not even a second story to run to. Robin pushes me behind her half-naked body, squares her shoulders, and swings open the bedroom door. I don't know if she thinks we're going to get caught anyway, so she might as well get it over with, or if she has a grandiose idea that she can finally win me in a standoff. I don't know if she thinks about what she's doing at all, but once she's opened the door, there's no turning back.

Chet is forced to take a couple of steps backward as Robin strides out of the bedroom and into the living room. I trail her, watching as Chet's eyes squeeze into slits. His shoulders hunch around his ears, his fists clench against his sides, and he takes a step toward her. I half run, half stumble to get in front of Robin and fall on my knees between them, my hands clasped prayer-like in front of me.

"Is this what you want?" Chet's veins bulge in his neck, but in his eyes, I see defeat as they swell with tears.

I begin to cry, too. What have I done? He's my high school boyfriend, my husband, Michael's father! How can I betray him like this?

"No, no, no." I sob at his feet.

Chet kicks his bat bag out of the way, pushes past Robin, and throws open the front door. Seemingly devoid now of the sadness he showed seconds before, he glowers over his shoulder at me.

"Take that off."

I look around me, confused.

"Take off *her* sweatshirt."

My face burns as I tug off the single piece of clothing I'm wearing. The sweatshirt barely clears my head when he rips it out of my hands and throws it at Robin.

"Get out!"

Robin's eyes never leave my face as she backs toward the doorway. "I love you, Lorinda," she chokes through her tears, muffled as she pulls on her sweatshirt.

Her eyes meet and stare into mine. I wordlessly beg her to forgive me for hurting her, for deserting her, for not *choosing* her.

"I said, get out!" Chet stomps toward Robin, and she tears down the porch stairs.

"If you ever come around here again, I'll kill you!" Chet slams the door.

Still on my knees, I collapse, prone on the floor, my naked body presses into the hardwood. Fleetingly, I imagine running after Robin, then running with her, but I can't muster the strength to lift my head. Maybe Satan will pull me through the gaps of the floorboards, straight to the gates of Hell.

"Get up," Chet says, stepping over me.

Somehow, I manage to wrap my arms around my naked body and labor to my feet. I follow Chet to our bedroom and shut the door behind me, hoping Michael will remain asleep in his room down the hall. I won't protest. I can't give Chet reason to disbelieve my sincerity in choosing to remain with him.

In one motion, he lifts me off my feet, onto the bed, and lands solidly on top of me. His body is heavy, I struggle to breathe from beneath him. I can't move, but he doesn't need anything from me. This is about his rage, his need to prove I belong to him, something I should never have forgotten. I'm his wife, his property, his, not mine. My body has never been mine and it never will be. Turning my head to one side, I leave the world below as I have a million times and float far above myself, counting, while Chet reclaims his territory.

On Monday, I learn Robin has quit the library. I'm unable to hide my devastation at the news. I wander aimlessly through my day; a constant rain of tears wets my cheeks. Jo asks how I'm doing, and, because I'm not sure if Chet's told her what happened, I try to put on a brave face. But I cry when Jo wraps her arms around me.

"Now, I have nothing," I sob into her shoulder.

"Oh honey," she soothes.

She doesn't question the meaning behind my words, and I don't try to explain. But there's always been a special bond between us, and I often feel she understands me in ways my mom can't. For one, she isn't bound by the restraints of religion, and so she keeps an open mind, but I also wonder if she sees herself in me, if she recognizes a woman struggling to be seen, to be known, apart from her role as mother and wife.

"I'm here for you." Jo kisses my cheek, hands me a tissue.

I cry harder. Would she be as kind if she knew what I'd done? I'd cheated on her son; I hardly deserved her sympathy. I force a smile, assure her I'll be fine, and head back to the shipping room. I slump into my chair and turn to look at Robin's desk. How can she be gone?

I don't drive directly home from work at the end of my workday. Instead, I drive to Robin's apartment, walk up to her porch, and pound on the door. I don't think about what I'm doing; I just know I have to talk to her, have to tell her I still love her, and that I'm sorry. Robin's brother answers the door.

"What do you want?" His upper lip curls into a snarl.

He stands at least seven inches above my five-foot-five-inch frame. I've only met him once before. He stays with Robin sometimes when he's on leave from the Army.

"I just want to talk to her."

"Don't you think you've done enough?" He spits chew from the bulge in his lower lip.

Brown liquid hits the step next to my shoe. He wipes his mouth with the back of his hand, starts to close the door.

"Wait!" My eyes fill with tears; his expression softens slightly.

"Look," he says, stepping out and closing the door behind him. "She's not here and if you know what's good for you, you'll turn around and never come back." He turns, hesitates, faces me again, "Whatever made you two women think you could be together? You have a husband, for Christ's sake!"

I cover my mouth with both of my hands, turn, and run back to my car. I wriggle behind the steering wheel, glance longingly over my shoulder, and whisper goodbye to Robin's bedroom window.

eight

Life with Chet goes on as if he never uncovered my infidelity, as if he never found me with Robin. He doesn't throw my transgression in my face or threaten me, he treats me as he always has, which triggers both relief and trepidation. Adultery is one sin in which our religion permits divorce, but having caught me in a homosexual act only fortifies Chet's position. I don't deserve the second chance he's affording me. Consequently, I know I ought to tread lightly. Mom's words of rebuke echo loudly in my ears, "Lorinda, you know better." And she's right. Since I was a little girl in Sunday school, I've been taught to keep myself pure for marriage. I came into my marriage stained, and now I've further corrupted myself. The only way to hold my longings for Robin at bay is to fully submerge myself into my faith. In obedience to this knowledge, I study my bible daily, pray, and meditate on God's words. I even convince Chet to host our church's small group meetings in our house, hopeful that communing with like-minded couples will support my efforts.

The couples in our group are kindhearted, spiritually whole-some, and bearing children at what I deem to be an alarming rate. No sooner does a woman wean one baby and she's pregnant again. I have no idea how these women hold everything together; some days, I can scarcely manage my *one* child. I finally feel I'm beginning to reclaim some freedom now that Michael is nearly four and much more independent. I'm not totally keen on sacri-ficing that independence to care for another baby. But when Chet begins pressing for more kids, I remind myself that this is God's will, and being a mother is the worthiest role a Christian woman is called to.

I agree to quit taking my birth control pills, and a couple of months later, my breasts are so tender I can't bear to wrap a bath towel around my chest. I know I'm pregnant again and immedi-ately my mind darkens with fear. When I miss my period for the second month in a row, I take a pregnancy test. The vivid pink plus-sign appears within seconds. I inform Chet of the positive reading, and he's elated.

He whoops and hollers and hugs Michael, "You're going to be a big brother!"

Chet's glee only serves to intensify my guilt at not feeling the same way. Still, I do my best to stifle my lack of enthusiasm and prepare for my second baby. I shop at thrift stores for onesies and bibs, rearrange Michael's tiny bedroom to make room for a crib, and even start to research names. When Michael inquires after his future sibling, I answer with what I hope sounds like authentic an-ticipation. I scold myself for my ungratefulness, reminding myself of the blessing of bringing forth a new life. Then, near the tail end of my fourth month of pregnancy, I hustle into the bathroom to pee. I pull down my pajama bottoms, and blood spills from the crotch of my pants, pooling on the floor. Strong waves of nausea and piercing abdominal cramps cause me to double over. I yell for Chet, and he helps me to the floor as I pass out.

For women who know they are pregnant, ten-to-fifteen percent end in miscarriage. Miscarriages are not uncommon. The more women you speak with, the more you realize how true this is. But I don't talk to these women and even if I did, I would still believe I killed my unborn baby. My disappointment in my pregnancy caused my baby's death; this is the only answer I can accept. In the hospital, I undergo a dilation and curettage procedure, and even though my doctor assures me the procedure is necessary to prevent infection, I'm terrified God will view this as an abortion. Not a year earlier, I marched in our local "Walk for Life," along with a couple hundred devoted Christian followers through the streets of downtown, holding signs reading "Abortion is Murder!" and "Save God's Unborn Children!" Now I lay with my legs in stirrups awaiting the dismembering and scraping out of my innocent baby's body. I'm a killer.

Though physically I heal quickly, emotionally I'm a wreck. The ache I feel inside is splitting me apart, and no amount of praying eases it. My doctor assures me three months after surgery that we are safe to start trying to get pregnant again. But I can't imagine moving past my loss. Losses—plural. Memories of Robin now plague my mind daily; I no longer have the will to drive them away. I'm forced to recognize that losing Robin has crushed me.

"How are you feeling these days?" The doctor asks at Michael's wellness check a few weeks later.

Michael picks a treat from the treasure chest; I shrug my shoulders. Accustomed to my silence, the doctor pats my shoulder. Michael holds a shiny fire truck sticker in one hand and a dinosaur eraser in the other.

"Mommy, can I have these?" He bobs with excitement.

I shake my head, ready to object to him taking two treats instead of one, but the doctor gives Michael a nod. Michael claps his closed fists together, twirls about.

"Lorinda, have I ever spoken to you about a therapist by the name of Michelle Beller?" He scratches her name and number on a piece of paper.

"The loss of a pregnancy can be difficult," he says, as he hands me the slip, "it's okay to ask for help."

"Our baby died." Michael shrugs his small shoulders as if asking a question rather than making a statement.

The doctor pats him on the head. Michael wraps his arms around my leg, I pick him up. The doctor sticks out his hand and I maneuver around Michael's wriggling body to shake it.

"You take care," he says.

Over the next couple of weeks, I take the doctor's note out of my purse a half-dozen times, but still, I don't call.

On my days off from the library, I settle Michael into his jogging stroller and roll him to the trail that leads to Whatcom Falls Park. From our house, the walk is about thirty minutes from the door to the falls. Michael points out every rabbit, squirrel, and deer he spots. He begs for me to stop and let him out to collect rocks, and often I do. The bite in the cool air, the roar of the water from the falls cascading off the cliffs and crashing into the lake below sends a jolt of energy into my soul. Temporarily, I feel hopeful. But eventually, not the solace of the forest, or the mighty thundering of Whatcom Falls is enough to keep me above water. Even the activities of daily living grow increasingly difficult, and soon I am unable to leave the house. I request and take leave from the library. Still, I can't bring myself to call the therapist. Michael is delighted to have me home all day. We eat peanut butter and jelly sandwiches while snuggling on the couch, watch television all day, and I even nap with him. Yet, as I hold him in my arms, breathing in his invigorating boyish scent, my exhaustion continues to worsen.

"Don't worry," Chet says, smoothing my hair with his palm, "we'll have another baby."

As if replacing loss is that simple, but I don't have the strength to protest.

My days and weeks merge into an unending flow of melancholy. If I could get away with it, I'd sit alone and just cry all day and night. I can't explain why I feel this way, I only know I do. Then, somewhere along the way, Chet resolves I will keep score for his softball team. I can think of nothing less appealing. Once, my evenings pulsated with the allure of burgeoning love and now . . . softball. But at his insistence, I can't deny I owe him at least this. And despite my resistance to the idea, I surprise myself by getting swept up in the excitement of the games. I even become adept at following the plays. Soon, I'm using scoring jargon like "fielder's choice," "double-play," and "sacrifice." Chet laughs more and jokes around with me during games. When he makes an impressive play, he runs into the dugout to kiss me. Sometimes, he picks me up and swings me around, which makes the guys whoop and holler. Chet seems proud to be with me. I feel more connected to him, more a part of his world.

Nearly a year has passed since the miscarriage, and still I haven't missed a single period. And, as it turns out, having intercourse even for the goal of making a baby isn't any more pleasurable for me than when we weren't trying. Still, my diligence pays off, and I miss a period. My breasts are already exceedingly sensitive, so I'm certain I'm pregnant by the time I make an appointment with the doctor.

After ticking off the usual questions about my last period, how many pregnancies I've had, and if I'm currently using birth control, the nurse excuses herself, leaving me with a cup to pee in. I hand Chet my purse and take my plastic cup down the hall to the bathroom. There's no convenient way to pee in a cup, not that I've found. No matter how I try not to, I end up peeing on my hand. I fill the cup, wipe it down with the alcohol wipes, and place it in the two-way pickup window.

When the nurse returns with the news that the pregnancy hormone, HCG, has been found in my urine, I simultaneously feel a wave of panic and relief. Relief at my evidence of acceptance back into God's good grace, relief at the chance I'll have a reprieve from sex, and panicked at the prospect of having another child to care for. Chet and I are reassured that a healthy fetus won't be affected by sexual intercourse. The doctor chuckles when he gives us permission to have sex for as long as is comfortable. I want to punch him in the face for saying so in front of Chet; pregnancy is supposed to be my respite. This time around, I find myself frequently nauseated, and I'm able to hold Chet at bay with the fear I'll vomit on him. Near the second trimester, my queasiness finally subsides. One afternoon, after Michael goes down for a nap, I'm leaning against the kitchen counter folding towels. I hear Chet come through the front door but don't call out as I don't want to wake Michael. Chet walks the dozen steps or so from the front door to where I stand in the kitchen and wraps his arms around me from behind.

"Hey," he kisses the top of my head.

I turn, breathe in the fragrance of his soap and aftershave. I relax into him. Chet's powerful chest and strong arms as he pulls me into him feel both gentle and protective. I close my eyes, comfortable in his embrace.

"Michael down for a nap?" I open my eyes to his seductive wink.

Ugh, the last thing I want is that! I nod hesitantly and he slips his hands under my shirt. I twist away from him.

"Ah, come on," he moans, pulling his hands from my shirt, and reaching for my head.

"Just give me a blowjob then."

I rear my head against his hand. "Stop!"

"*Geez*, sorry." Chet throws his hands up in surrender and stomps away.

I fight back tears, return my attention to folding towels. Why do all physical interactions with him have to end up being sexual? I want him to hold me, to emotionally connect with me. Is that too much to ask? Maybe. Maybe it is. I know right away I've hurt Chet's feelings or pride or both. I know I should make it up to him, but I don't want to. I'm tired of sexually pleasing him with no regard to whether I derive pleasure from the experience. And I loathe feeling like a human trash can for his semen. I'm pregnant and don't feel like having sex; don't my feelings matter? But I know they don't. My place is to submit to my husband, pregnant or not. I fold the last towel and return the laundry basket to the utility room behind our bedroom. Chet is stretched across the bed looking at a magazine. I roll my shoulders back, take in a deep breath, and lie down next to him. He puts down his magazine and I reach for the zipper on his jeans.

nine

Spring melts into summer, and warmer temperatures, combined with longer days, bring more softball. Often, after weekend games, ball players and their families hang out together in the park to barbecue. I appreciate the break these gatherings afford me, as Michael wants to stay right at his dad's side, and Chet is normally accommodating. Once I lay out a blanket, staking our lunch spot, I make eye contact with Chet. I motion toward the trail, indicating I'm going for a walk around the lake. He gives me a half nod and I take off. The fresh air, combined with the jovial sounds of picnickers, has me feeling invigorated. Halfway into my second trimester, I appear softer than normal but not visibly pregnant. Of course, I make a conscious effort not to gain more weight than necessary. Walking is my primary exercise, but I also work out at the gym most days. Three-quarters of the way around the lake, my forehead is damp with sweat and my breathing is labored. I veer off the trail to rest against a huge fir tree. I flatten my lower back into the trunk, lean my head back, and shut my eyes. The woodsy scent of pine trees mixed with fire-roasted hot dogs wafts on the breeze, bringing back memories of camping with Robin. My mind conjures up the smoothness of her lips pressing to my cheek. If only I could make her real right now. I mentally drift away. A branch breaks somewhere behind me, then what feels like a hand brushes the back of my thigh. I whip my head around and come face-to-face with Russ. He's a pickup player one of the guys has found to fill in for an injured teammate. Russ smells of beer, I suck in my breath. He grins, displaying yellow teeth peppered with flecks of dark, grainy chewing tobacco. He reaches for my arm, but I slap at him. Russ cocks his head, and spits a brown wad of saliva and tobacco on the ground, barely missing my sandal. Then, he seizes me around my waist, and my first thought is of my baby. I shove him hard in retaliation and he stumbles backwards.

"Bitch." He opens his arms wide, shrugs, signaling he's letting me go; I'm free.

My feet remain planted and I stare back at him. I take in his grungy baseball hat pulled low over his eyes, his untucked T-shirt, and grass-stained sweats. He has oversized, dirty hands and bulky shoulders, and he's just a pathetically drunk, stupid man. As I take him in, picking him apart one limb, one shabby piece of clothing at a time, my fear shrivels like a slug doused in salt, and from deep inside, my usually absent voice bubbles up and out in a scathing tone.

"You don't tell *me* when to go!" The rage I hold so close, usually turn inward, now erupts.

He gapes at me wide-eyed as I march forward and press my chest against his, knocking him aggressively into the tree trunk behind him. He throws his arms in the air in mock resignation and smirks. I yank his sweats down to his ankles. He draws in a shocked breath as I land clumsily on my knees in front of him and cram his dick into my mouth. When he moans, I pull him deeper down my throat, his veins bulge against my lips. I contemplate biting him and the idea almost makes me laugh. He ejaculates within seconds; I spit the whole wad on his foot. I stand, brush the dirt from my knees.

"Fuck you." The words I rarely dare say aloud tumble from my lips like old friends.

I feel invincible, emboldened. I leave him limp against the tree with his pants down. By the time we're headed home from the park, my exhilaration has begun to wear off. And when I climb into bed that night, the condemning voices in my head rage louder and more fiercely than ever before.

The next morning, I roll across the bed into the warm spot left behind by Chet. I bury my face in his pillow, breathe in the scent of his shampoo. My husband, father of my children, what have I done? How can I have betrayed him again? The tears rush to my eyes, soaking his pillow. I consider smothering myself. Michael is making noise from his bedroom and I know I should go to him. I roll onto my back and stare at the ceiling. A crack in the plaster is swirled in the shape of an S. "S" for sinner. I grab Chet's pillow and press it against my face. I hold my breath, suck the pillowcase fabric into my nostrils, wait. Wait for blackness, for weightlessness, for nothingness. *Do not breathe.*

"Mommy!" Michael's voice cuts through my silence, I hurl into consciousness.

Fuck. I dangle one leg out of bed, skimming the cold floor with my foot. I shimmy my body closer to the edge of the mattress, let myself slip all the way down to the freezing tile.

"Mommy!" I crawl to my feet and waddle into the hall.

My protruding belly presses noticeably against my T-shirt. Did I grow bigger overnight? The recollection of my obscene act of the day before fills my heart with shame and my mouth with too much saliva. I turn quickly into the bathroom, just barely flipping up the toilet seat in time. I gag on phlegm and bile, my nose drips with snot as I vomit.

"Mom!" Michael is banging on his bedroom door from inside his room.

Nothing is preventing him from opening it and walking out, but still, he wails and pounds. I flush the toilet.

"Back up, Michael," I warn, not wanting to knock him down with his bedroom door as I push it open.

He holds his stuffed gray-and-white shark in one hand, his blanket in the other, his face red with exertion.

"Sorry, buddy." I kneel and wrap him in my arms.

"Hi baby," he says cheerfully to my stomach as if he has not just been desperately shouting for me.

My eyes well up as I feel Michael's warm hand patting his future sibling, and I know I can't check out.

After my encounter with Russ in the woods, I recognize my need for outside help. In the bottom of my purse is the wadded piece of paper with the therapist's number given to me by my doctor. I fish out the paper, flatten it under my palm, and dial the number. When a recorded voice answers, I'm relieved. I have no idea what to say. I listen to the options, choose the answering machine for Michelle Beller-Siegfried, and leave my name and phone number. The following week, I sit perched on the edge of her leather couch, self-consciously rubbing my hands over my marginally protruding belly. The Beller, as I've mentally begun to refer to her, rocks back and forth in her rocker. Her long skirt balloons, then deflates with the motion. Strands of beaded glass chime against one another from around her neck and a turquoise head-band bursts at its seams to hold secure her defiant hair. She appears bright and happy, in complete contrast to my despair. I stumble awkwardly through the basics: my name, date of birth, marital status, and the fact that I'm a mother of one and expecting another. I soon discover those are the easiest questions I'll be asked.

"Why do you think your doctor referred you?" She smiles warmly.

I fiddle with a loose thread hanging from the hem of my shirt. I'm unravelling. "He believes I'm unhappy."

"Do you think you deserve unhappiness, Lorinda?"

Do I deserve it? That seems an odd way to ask the question, but after what I've done, unhappiness seems mild punishment. I nod from behind the protective curtain of my long hair.

"Why?"

Shit. She won't get it; she won't understand what I've done is not only unacceptable in the secular world, but worthy of eternal death in the Christian world. Maybe coming here was a mistake. I know better than to have sought help from a counselor outside of the church. The Beller pulls her glasses off, lays them in her lap. I rub my forehead with my palms. Like looking through a View-Master, I click through the slides of my life, from Chet to Robin to the birth of Michael to my current pregnancy, and then to the guy in the woods. Why won't words simply shake loose and land decipherably on my tongue?

"Lorinda, where are you right now?"

The rocking of the Beller's chair, like the ticking of a clock, beats a rhythm through my wandering mind, pulls me back to the present. I shift, smooth my extra-long shirt over my legs.

"Talking can be difficult. How do you feel about writing?" She selects a pen and pad of paper from her desk, holds them out to me. I take them. Heat flows from a space heater in the corner of the room, but my fingers feel frigid. I force them around the pen, scribble my most honest response, then hand the paper to the Beller. She puts on her glasses.

"I do not think there could be anyone in this world that despises me more than I do. If I were a better person, I wouldn't be so unhappy." The Beller reads my words aloud and I feel my cheeks burn hot with embarrassment. *Who even talks like that? Why can't I just be normal?*

"Why do you despise yourself?" The Beller doesn't react to my dramatic writing.

"I deserve to go to Hell," I reply, not answering her question.

Without taking her eyes off me, the Beller slowly begins to rock again.

"And why do you think you deserve Hell?" Her eyes are warm, but a curly wisp of her hair springs out from under her headband, pointing accusingly in my direction.

I don't have an answer for her I can articulate. I let my eyes blur, my mind drifts away. I float above the Beller, above myself.

She hands me the pad of paper. "Write down your feelings, whatever comes to mind," I hear her say. "Bring it back next week."

Though I plan to stuff the tablet in a drawer and pull it out the day of the next appointment, I fill most of it within the first couple of hours I'm home. I'm surprised by how effortlessly the words flow. The more I write, the more I have to say. Tears roll off my cheeks and hit the paper, smearing the ink, but I keep writing. I feel physically lighter as my truth bleeds out of me and onto the paper. When my hand is cramped into a claw, I quit writing and hide the pad of paper under a stack of photo albums in the bookcase.

During the night, in bed next to Chet, I think about the hidden tablet, about the horrendous truths I've admitted to. The only way for me to cope is to push the thoughts away, secure them into a box in the furthest part of mind, only to be brought out when I see the Beller. Chet doesn't know about counseling. I don't have a particular reason to keep the Beller a secret, but I like having this one thing, this one person kept to myself. I know he will eventually find out, because our medical insurance bills will show her name as treatment being covered for me. There's no way I could see her without insurance. Therapy isn't a necessity, especially since I have access to God and my church family at any time, and they are free, but the Beller doesn't have rigid, preconceived ideas of how I should behave. I'm drawn to her soothing voice and gentle manner. I don't know her religious beliefs, but I get the feeling they aren't doctrinaire like mine.

Upon our second visit, the Beller asks for the tablet. I hand it to her. She reads as I fidget, picking at the frayed skin around my thumbnail. When she's finished, she looks at me. I flush under her gaze and silently pray she doesn't say anything.

"Lorinda," the Beller scoots her rocker closer to me, "this is good writing."

I can't help but smile. I do love to write.

"How did you feel writing this?"

She has such a kind voice. I wish I could answer her. I shrug.

"Well, don't stop writing," she says, "If this is how you are able to share with me, then this is what we will do. You will talk when you are ready."

I feel a tremendous weight lift from shoulders. "Oh, thank you," I say to myself as I pray silently to God.

Each week, upon seeing the Beller, I feel a flutter of hope as she relieves me of the burden of my secrets. She reads about my uncle, the girl I kissed in sixth grade, and the man in the woods. I write of my religious upbringing, how I'd always known God was watching and how dirty this made me feel. I've penned in the least incriminating way I can find to describe what happened between me and Robin and Chet; still, my face burns as I watch her read. Dread consumes me as I imagine my sins and secrets no longer hidden, the inky words leaking from the paper, pooling, exposed, onto the floor.

After reading several pages of my writing, the Beller looks up at me.

"And this is why you think you will go to hell?" She doesn't sound condescending or angry, just genuinely interested.

I nod.

"There's a lot to unpack here, and if you are willing, I am here to help you."

I bury my head in my hands. An unbearable pressure thuds against my skull, an instant headache. I want to tell her how lonely I am for Robin, but how horrible I feel about cheating on Chet. I'm also just so embarrassed, so ashamed. When I finally look up, she's holding out a Kleenex box. I take several, wipe at mascara streaks and my runny nose.

"There is something I would like to ask you. Have you considered maybe you'd rather be with women and not men?" She angles her head to the side, waits.

"No," I sputter.

"You haven't?"

"I mean, yes. But no, I can't." I shake my head as if trying to rid myself of the thought.

"Why can't you?" The Beller leans slightly forward.

"Because that's not allowed. I could never . . ." Am I trying to convince myself or her?

"What would happen if you decided to leave Chet?" The Beller pushes me, and I'm not sure I like it.

I shake my head again and close my eyes. She doesn't understand, and this is where I recognize our differences in beliefs are significant. I have no answer for her, but she shoves the tablet and pen in my direction. I don't accept either; I've lost my words, and I cannot find them even to write them down.

ten

October 9, 1999, Taylor is born, weighing six pounds and twelve ounces, every bit a normal-sized, healthy baby. I'm up, showered, and ready to go home the day after he is born. He's a cuddly baby but doesn't like to sleep apart from me. We spend many hours in the rocking chair. Each time I gaze into Taylor's cobalt eyes, I vow to myself, to God, that I will never stray from my marriage again. I feel the weight of my responsibilities heavy on my heart and I know I will never put my marriage at risk again.

I give up my job at the library the day Taylor is born and about a month later, I begin on a new job path in fitness. I teach classes at a nearby gym in the mornings before Chet leaves for work. When Taylor is old enough, I bring the boys with me and use the daycare provided. The job is flexible; I can work around Chet's schedule, and, despite my shyness, when I step in front of a fitness class, I become a completely different person. For the first time, I feel I've found something I'm profoundly good at. I find a voice in front of my classes I'm often too timid to share elsewhere in my life. And unlike my brazen alter-ego in the woods, this voice is one I can be proud of. I find another bonus of the job is how it ups my mood. On the days I don't teach at the gym, I take the boys for a walk.

One afternoon, I decide to wander into town rather than down the trail that snakes through the park to Whatcom Falls. Taylor sleeps soundly in the jogging stroller while Michael points out every bird he spots. We near the city library and I'm struck with a pang of sadness. I roll the stroller past the front door, but slowly, as I gaze through the glass. Book trucks form aisles and I can see a line of patrons waiting at the front desk. I'm curious as to what new books might be out and consider rolling the stroller inside when I hear Michael shout gleefully. I follow his pointing finger, stuck out like a bird-dog tail, and see Robin leaning against a book dolly, having just unloaded the delivery truck. She smiles hesitantly. Michael tries to unbuckle himself from the stroller. Unwilling to further ignore Michael's enthusiasm, Robin abandons the dolly and approaches the stroller. She kneels and takes his hand in hers.

"Hey there, how've you been buddy?"

I can scarcely believe Michael remembers her. He hasn't seen her since he was two-and-a-half, a lifetime in a young child's life. But he's bubbling with excitement, rattling on about his new cars.

"You want to see?" he asks.

A familiar smile spreads across Robin's lips as she watches his face brighten with the idea. She looks to me. Our eyes meet and I'm dumbstruck, speechless, drowning in a torrent of memories and emotions. But Robin's expression gives nothing away. I look from her to the library and I'm confused. Has she been working all this time for the city library a couple of miles from my house? Michael kicks his heels against the stroller, waking Taylor. Robin reaches over and pulls the blanket away from Taylor's face. He lets out one quick cry and then immediately smiles, his cheeks dimpling at the corners. Robins stands, brushes off her knees. She leans close enough that I can smell the coffee on her breath and feel the heat radiating from her body.

"Now that you've had another baby, you'll never leave him. He has you." She grabs the dolly of books and wheels into the library, the heavy glass doors shut behind her.

Her words cut through me and I slip into a noticeable funk. Not full-on depression, but something skimming the top, for sure. From then on, I quit strolling the kids to the park and instead pass the city library as often as I can, hoping to spot Robin. Should I see her, I don't know what I'll say; she's made her feelings clear. She has as much as told me that we're through forever. I know this and I know it's in my best interest and hers, but that doesn't stop the ache I feel. I don't mention our chance meeting to the Beller, that would be moving backward. I'm finding my voice in therapy more often now, and since Taylor's birth, I've been living straight as an arrow.

To help in this endeavor, I clean our house in its entirety each morning before the kids are awake. I appreciate the sense of accomplishment, but I also begin to feel a bit suffocated. I have two kids, and with only two bedrooms and one bathroom, there is nowhere to hide for even a minute. I want to move. I'm surprised to find Chet is completely on board with the idea. Fortunately, the little house we paid $69,000 for in 1990 is now worth twice as much in 2000. Unfortunately, we've taken out a second mortgage to consolidate credit card debt, and even if we manage to sell our house for exactly what we ask, we still won't have enough for a down payment on a new house. Of course, that doesn't stop us from house-hunting all over town. We check out a gazillion different places. Our first stop is an extravagant residence we cannot possibly afford. The realtor unlocks the padlock, and we stroll through the massive double doors. Chet winks at me. His bulky arm flexes into a tight muscle, his little finger wiggles in the air as if holding a cup of tea. I can't help but giggle. The realtor looks up from the information on the clipboard he's using to read us the houses specs. Chet and I both shake our heads. We pile into the realtor's SUV. Chet slides his hand into mine, gives it a squeeze. We head to the next place on the list. Our mood is light, playful. Chet and I are enjoying our time together.

On days like this, I find it hard to imagine I've loved anyone other than Chet, that my heart has ever ached for Robin. When finally our realtor takes us to look at a year-old house built in a meticulous neighborhood, I fall in love. The house is two stories with three bedrooms and three baths. I stroll about in a delirious stupor, there's so much space! There's an attached garage, which means I can park my car inside. No more hauling groceries to the house in the rain or defrosting the windshield on chilly mornings. This is the kind of convenience that up until now had been a dream. All that's left is to figure out how to pay for it. And here's where the party ends; there just isn't a way financially to make it work. We need a more substantial down payment than what we have available. I try to reason with myself, tell myself that we can move someday when our finances are more together. But Chet isn't quite ready to throw in the towel, and, as a last resort, he asks his parents if we can borrow money from them. They are understandably hesitant. What if something goes wrong and we can't pay them back? They are on a semi-fixed budget. But Chet assures them that his job at the Alcoa aluminum smelter is solid, and, in the end, persuades them to loan us the money. This is our fresh beginning, a new house in a new neighborhood—everything will be better. I can feel it.

In 2003, less than two years after moving into our new house, Alcoa announces it will be laying off two hundred of the six hundred workers at the smelter and cutting production in half because of high electricity costs.

This is a setback we hadn't predicted and weren't financially prepared to navigate. Chet qualifies for the worker retraining program, which means he can attend community college free of charge to acquire skills for another job. But the program is two-to-three-years long, with no guarantee of a job at the end. Meanwhile, he collects unemployment and I increase my hours at the gym, but still, we can't fully make ends meet. We don't have money enough to pay back Chet's parents, but he assures me they understand.

This incredible stress and uncertainty causes me extreme anxiety. I have nightmares about our lovely new house filling with water, the walls sagging under the weight, then disintegrating and floating away. In my dreams, we end up back in our old house, but now it's in terrible condition and we no longer own it but rather we're forced to rent. My unease reaches new heights and not only in my dreams. I suspect something is up with Chet. More frequently, he's staying away from home past his usual school hours. When I question him, he claims he's studying. I want to believe him, to trust him, but something in the way he behaves is strange. The biggest tip-off should be that he's not expressing his usual persistent desire for sex, and as much as this is a relief, it also isn't.

"Hey, I'm heading over to study group," says Chet from under the baseball cap he's pulled down to his brows.

His flannel pajama bottoms cover the tops of his feet, exposing only his toes, which poke over the ends of his flip-flops. Books tucked under one arm, his other hand is jammed into the pocket of his sweatshirt.

"You're going to study group in your pajamas?" I question.

"It's informal. Besides, it's Saturday." He reaches for the garage door.

"Wait, we have family coming today," I yell at his disappearing back.

Our families are coming over to celebrate Chet's sister's graduation from college. There will most definitely be a house full, and I need his help. He raises his hand in recognition and gets into his car.

A few hours later, I have a ham simmering in the crockpot and a cake in the oven. I glance at the clock; surely Chet will return soon. But the time continues to tick away and thirty minutes before everyone is to arrive, I finally call his cell phone. He doesn't answer, my call goes directly to voicemail. He'd said he was going to a study group, so I scour the computer desk for his group's numbers. I find a list buried at the bottom of a messy stack of school notes and dial the first number.

"Who are you looking for?" a groggy voice asks.

"Chet."

"Uh, no. We aren't meeting today that I know of." He yawns.

I thank him and move down the list, but the answer is the same, no one is studying today, and no one has spoken to Chet. Our family is due to arrive any minute. I plop down in the desk chair. Where has he run off to in pajamas and flip-flops? I hear gravel crunching beneath tires and look out the window to see Chet's parents driving up.

"Hi hon'," Jo says, and greets me with a kiss on the cheek. Her eyes dart around the room.

"He should be here any minute," I say in answer to her un-asked question.

My parents arrive next, but before I have a chance to greet them, Chet bursts through the kitchen door and darts upstairs. Both sets of parents turn to watch him, then their eyes settle on me. I have no idea what to tell them, no idea where he's been or what he's doing now. I excuse myself, take the steps two at a time and swing into our bedroom. Chet's locked himself in the bath-room.

"Hey!" I yell from outside the door.

"Be right there!" he calls over the sound of the shower.

"Where were you?" I try to keep the frustration out of my voice.

He opens the door. "I told you. I was studying."

He pushes past me to the dresser and forcefully begins open-ing and slamming drawers. He pulls out shorts and a tank top, and starts getting dressed.

"I called everyone on your study group list. Who were you with, Chet?"

He whips around to face me, "Hey cheater, you have no right to accuse me."

His words hit like daggers. My shame at what occurred between Robin and me weighs as heavy now as when it happened.

"That was a long time ago and I've told you I'm sorry."

The very foundation of our faith is built on forgiveness. The Bible says in Psalm 103:12, "As far as the east is from the west, so far has He removed our transgressions from us." We are commanded to follow the words in the Bible, to forgive one another as God forgave us. Chet must know how repentant I am by now. Can't he see how hard I've tried to prove my loyalty to him?

"Oh, I see," he sneers. "You say you're sorry and I'm just supposed to forget?" His face contorts in anger.

"What do you want me to say?" I reach out to touch him, but he pulls away.

"Nothing!" He huffs off and I sink onto the bed.

I can hear Chet greeting everyone downstairs. Can hear my dad clap him on the shoulder, the laughter of our kids. I half hope Chet *has* cheated on me. After the chaos I've caused in our marriage and the detrimental effects my unfaithfulness has obviously had on him, it's what I deserve. I wipe my eyes, blow my nose, and head downstairs. I smile, converse, and pretend that nothing has gone wrong because maybe nothing has.

That night, when Chet lays down next to me in bed, before he even utters a word, I know I'm right about him having an affair.

"She doesn't mean anything to me," he whispers. "I told her I couldn't see her again."

I feel sick to my stomach. I don't even want to think of his hands on another woman's body. The idea doesn't only make me sick; it makes me mad. I want to kick him in the leg, the jerk. He cheated on me! I flip back the blankets. I can't sleep next to him! I grab my pillow and plod downstairs. I hurl my pillow at the couch, pick it up and hurl it again.

"Asshole!" I scream silently.

I flop back onto the couch, cover my face with my pillow and scream. My screams turn to sobs and I wonder how we ever arrived at this place. We pledged our hearts, our bodies, to each other. But I betrayed him first. I took his love for granted. I know I have only myself to blame. I must do better, be better, try harder.

In May of 2006, Alcoa calls Chet back to his job at the smelter, which I consider a miracle, as we're dangerously close to emptying our bank account. In the three years he's been laid off, Chet's earned an associate degree as well as a certificate in computer programming. He'd hoped to find a job in computers, but nothing has come along. So, he accepts his old job at the smelter and life returns to normal. I begin to feel more settled as our financial burdens lessen.

Taylor has grown from a rambunctious toddler to an even more active kindergartener. Michael is now a happy third-grader. I continue to teach classes and train clients at the gym. And at home, I focus my attention more intentionally on Chet.

One morning, I awake before my alarm clock, get dressed, and sprint down the porch steps to meet my running partner, Tara, a woman I ran a marathon with in 1998. We've remained friendly over the years, but reconnected and became running partners when I moved to the new house. She has her heel propped up on the bumper of her car, reaching for her toes and stretching her hamstrings. When she sees me, she swings her leg down. We hug in greeting, then take off for the trail. Tara is a quick runner, faster than me, and keeping up with her is a challenge, but I manage to hold up my end of a conversation. Most mornings, Tara and I aren't gone longer than an hour. Still, Chet is ready to bolt out the door for work as soon as we arrive. So, when we push open the front door that morning, I'm surprised to see Chet rummaging through the junk drawer in the kitchen.

"Hey," I say, continuing past him and following Tara upstairs.

Since Tara lives about eleven miles away in the next town but works in this one, she often showers at our house to save herself time. I lay out a clean towel for her, then scurry back downstairs. Chet's lunch box sits on the kitchen counter, but he's nowhere to be found. I wonder if he's lost his keys, if I should ask him if he needs my help. I call his name, but he doesn't answer, and I don't find him anywhere on the first floor. I fill two mugs with coffee and head back upstairs. I balance both cups and push at the corner of the bedroom door with my toes. The door swings open. Chet is lying prostrate on the floor holding a mirror under the door, straining to get a glimpse of my naked friend. I gasp out loud.

"Chet! What the . . ."

Caught like a wild animal in headlights, he stares at me, all glassy-eyed from his position on the ground. Without saying a word, he scrambles to his feet, tosses the mirror under our bed, and tears past me out of the bedroom. Tara opens the bathroom door and a blast of steamy air slaps me in the face. I stand immobile as a scarecrow on the other side, clinging to the mugs of hot coffee.

"Wow, thanks!" She takes a cup from me. "What service!"

I force a smile, a head nod. I perch on the edge of my bed, eyes focused on the contents of my own mug of dark, black coffee, the color of impending doom. Tara makes small talk, but I comprehend nothing of what she says.

Once she's gone, I dump my untouched coffee, now cold, down the drain and start a fresh pot. The sun shines through the kitchen, I stare blankly out the window. We have been doing so well. We even have "Naked Tuesdays," on the Tuesdays Chet doesn't go into work until late. After we drop the boys at school, we come back home, have sex, then stretch out naked in bed and watch movies until he leaves for work. Although lately, Tuesdays have been the *only* day we have sex all week, and some interruptions have messed those days up, too. The kids' early dismissal from school and appointments I can't schedule for any other day except Tuesday have interfered, but certainly, he's noticed the effort I've been making. Or have I only imagined things between us were improving? I can only conclude he's been lured into temptation because I'm not sexually fulfilling him.

Michael and Taylor clamber down the stairs, I realize I haven't even begun to fry eggs or toast bread. I pull a box of pop tarts out of the cupboard. My cell phone buzzes, and I flip it open. Text messages from Chet flood in. The first couple, apologetic in tone, quickly take on an accusatory tone as he blames me for becoming too busy to fulfill his sexual needs, thus confirming my own self-recrimination. The memory of him on the floor with the mirror flashes across my mind, making the hair on my neck stand up. Chet's unfaithfulness is my fault, just as I'd always believed what my uncle did was my fault, too. But I know this is different, because I *owe* sexual fulfillment to Chet, or so I tell myself. So, before the end of his workday, I text Chet an apology.

Less than two weeks after the mirror incident, Tara informs me she must quit running. I feel my face grow hot with shame and embarrassment, as I prepare to apologize for what Chet has done. I don't know where to begin or how she's found out. But as I deliberate over what to say next, I hear her say she's developed pain in her feet. Her doctor has diagnosed her with tarsal tunnel syndrome, and because of other issues with her feet, has been told she shouldn't run again. My first thought is relief that she's still ignorant of Chet's leering. Then I cry, and she cries, and we promise to get together for a bike-ride. I know if we aren't running daily, our connection will ease off and eventually fade. We don't live in the same town or work at the same job, our kids aren't buddies, so we will drift apart.

I continue to run alone, going out later in the day when it's light. I recognize the correlation between my mental health and running, so I know better than to quit. But I'd relished the closeness I felt with Tara and I miss our conversations. I long to feel joined to someone, to feel whole. I can't explain the emptiness in my heart, or the unrest in my mind, but both cause me actual physical pain. Tara gave up running for her own well-being, completely unrelated to anything I've done, and still, I feel rejected, alone.

At the gym, I find a flyer advertising a local running club. For a small yearly fee, I can participate in at least one local race each month. This idea appeals to me, so I work up the nerve and join. I soon find familiar faces, clients, and coworkers from the gym I work for. Aaron's been faithfully attending my fitness classes for years. He's a runner, and the rumor around the gym is that he's fast. I've seen him at races, but only briefly, as he takes off while I'm left bumping along toward the back of the pack. So, I'm more than a little surprised when, as I kneel to tie my shoelace, he sidles up and asks if he can run next to me. *Why?* I'm certainly not as fast as he is. But he's persistent, and finally I agree. I find him to be witty and clever, I laugh nearly the entire run. When we reach the finish line, I turn to him and blurt, "Do you have a running partner?"

He grins back at me. "I do now."

My intention to live as a godly wife is sincere; I vow I'll never again lose sight of my marital obligations. But running daily with Aaron lessens my depression, lifts my overall sense of well-being, and I get comfortable, loosen up on expectations I've put on myself. The changes are subtle, or they are for me, and I may have even gone on without noticing. Until one night, as I use Chet's side of the sheet to wipe away what he's left behind, I hear him snap, "You could at least pretend to be interested."

He rolls off the bed and stomps into the bathroom. I hear the shower door slam behind him, feel a weight drop in my stomach. When he emerges from the bathroom, a towel wrapped around his waist, I hustle to give him a kiss. But he spins away from me and out of our bedroom, no doubt heading to sleep on the couch. Panic, regret, fear all roil and toss in my gut and I battle with whether to follow him or not. In the end, I choose not to. I stay in bed, willing sleep to ease my anxiety.

The next morning, I get up and dress quietly into my running clothes. I scoop up my cell phone from my bedstand and habitually flip it open.

"I'm not even going to try to touch you anymore. If you want to have sex, you will have to initiate it. I'm done. I'm sick of you making me feel like some monster. Why do you even want to be with me at all? I'm just done trying with you . . ." Chet's angry texts fill the screen. I glance at his side of the bed, empty.

An arctic chill holds me frozen in place and I imagine myself caught again, weak, pathetic, naked on the floor, begging at Chet's feet for forgiveness. His words from the night before rush back. I tiptoe downstairs to where he snores soundly on the family room couch, afghan stretched tightly around him. I study his face, his forever smooth, tan skin, the shiny black of his hair splayed over his forehead, I know this man's body. Every dip and rise of his shape, every scar and dimple. I do love him. What I don't identify is that my love for him is maternal, not unlike the love I have for my boys. I should skip running with Aaron, stay with Chet, apologize, make it up to him. But I don't. Instead, I slip quietly out the front door, run quickly down the driveway to where Aaron waits at the trail's entrance. He smiles, nods, and we take off.

For the first mile or so as we zigzag in and out of thick masses of trees, we speak little. Our feet pound out a rhythm as they hit the twisty rock-and-dirt trail. We reach a spot where the trail turns into a bridge that arches over the road. We run to the middle of the bridge, where we stop and lean against the railing. The sun reaches out with bright rays of light as it rises, sparkling against the sleeping city. Past the houses and buildings, we can just catch a glimpse of Bellingham Bay. The air bites at my exposed nose and freezes on my damp lips. I feel warmth from Aaron's hand as it settles on the small of my back. I don't pull away; I don't want to move at all. For a moment, I forget Chet, forget my short-comings, and I feel at peace with the world, with myself.

"Brilliant," Aaron marvels.

I nod in agreement, taking advantage of the short break to catch my breath. Sooner than I'd like, he readjusts his hat, looks back at me with a wink, and takes off running again. His strong calves flex as his feet hit the ground, his stride is strong, sure. No matter how many miles we run, his posture remains enviable; chest high, shoulders back, and lifted through the rib cage. In contrast, as I grow tired, I roll, collapse into myself like a pill bug, unable to suck in a deep breath. We pick up the pace, sprint briskly up a slight hill, the gravel crunching beneath our feet. We wind through the thick forest; the trail begins to level out and narrow. Aaron slows and I plow teasingly into the back of him. Abruptly, he whirls around, whisks me off the trail and into the dense concealment of the fir trees. He pulls me into him, kisses me hard on the mouth, the saltiness of his lips burning into mine. My first inclination is to panic, until I feel him hardening against my thigh. Then, without warning, the fearless woman I'd been in the woods a few years earlier awakens inside. Instead of pulling away, I provoke him by matching his urgency until there's nothing left to do but fuck. He digs into his jacket, pulls out a condom, I don't stop him. Sweat drips from the brim of his hat onto my cheek. His gorgeous brown eyes, feathered by long, luscious eye-lashes blink excitedly as he rips open the package. He's beautiful, and I'm certain plenty of women would love to have sex with him—though maybe not up against a tree. He's thoughtful enough to put his hand between my head and the tree trunk as he rams into me from behind. The sex is rough, maybe even angry, and I'm reminded of my inclination to bite the man in the woods. Aaron comes before I have time to process how we've gone from running to screwing. I don't orgasm, but I do experience a release. A high, an intoxication so potent I feel my body morph from the weak, insignificant girl I believe myself to be into the powerful, capable woman I long to be.

"Was it okay?" he asks. We adjust our clothing; he tosses the oozing condom behind him. I sense he needs something from me. Maybe assurance that he's performed with the panache he'd intended; I'm not sure. What I know is that with this man, like the man in the woods, I have power.

When we return to where we started, I say goodbye and fly toward my house. I leap up the steps of my front porch. Drunk, high on adrenaline, I surge through the front door. Chet is leaning against the kitchen counter drinking a cup of coffee.

"How was your run?" He holds a steaming mug for me.

His tone is soft, apologetic, he's holding out the olive branch. Me? I've just banged my running partner. And just like that, I collide once again with reality. My euphoria evaporates, replaced by dark self-hatred.

eleven

The Beller stops rocking, pulls herself closer to the leather couch. "Lorinda, do you want to be married?"

I smell peppermint tea on her breath, my stomach growls. I can't remember when I last ate anything of substance. I'm too anxious to eat. Hugging the afghan around me like an oversized shawl, I inhale, pull my belly in as hard as I can, then exhale. The Beller waits, unmoved, for my response.

"Of course I want to be married," I write on my tablet before sinking back into the couch.

I've written the words quickly, too quickly, because they're the words I've been programmed to write. In truth, I cheat on Chet, tell Aaron we're through, then swear I'll never cheat again. But I do cheat again because I'm now hostage to the ensuing junkie high, false sense of control, and power. As a result, I inadvertently distance myself from Chet, going as far as to scoot away from him in bed at night, pretending to be asleep. When we do have sex, I don't conjure images of the man in the woods or Aaron, I summon the memory of Robin. Even now, nearly a decade after our affair, I ache for her. I recall the sensual touch of her hands cupping my breasts, slipping between my thighs, the heat of her breath on my skin, the pulse of our hearts beating in unison, and I realize losing her has torn a hole inside me. I haven't left her behind at all.

I pen what I believe to be appropriate rather than true: "I want to be the kind of wife God wants me to be. The kind of wife Chet deserves."

The Beller holds out her hand and I offer her the tablet. She reads my words aloud, but I barely recognize them, for they are the words of the righteous woman I've failed to be.

I don't visit the Beller regularly. Trusting her to lead me in the right direction may be reckless, but how can I admit who I truly am to anyone from church? I'm unravelling at a pace too fast to stop, I know I need someone, so it's the Beller I turn to. What I really want to admit is how hopelessly, forever in love I am with Robin, and that given the opportunity without consequence, I'd choose to be with her. But I don't. I write only about Aaron because I believe having an affair with him to be a more acceptable thing to admit than wanting to be with Robin. I'm not fooling the Beller. She may be gentle and quiet, but she's also extremely perceptive. When our hour has ticked away, I stand, and she lays her hand on mine.

"My intention is to listen, Lorinda, not to judge."

I nod. *See me! Hear me! Help me!* But how can she if I won't let her in? I leave her office, walk to the car. I wonder why I bother to see the Beller at all. I also wonder how much longer I can fight my darkness before I choose to check out of this life for good.

The next morning, I hurriedly step from the shower, droplets of water dripping down my back as I gather my hair into a wet ponytail. I pull on jeans, yank a T-shirt over my head. Fog clouds the bathroom mirror; I hurriedly wipe it away. I quickly outline my eyes with eyeliner and brush my lashes with waterproof mascara. With less than an hour to get the kids out of the house to their respective schools, there's no time to waste. Michael and Taylor run into my bathroom squawking about whose turn it is to feed the cats. I hand them each a scoop and position them in front of the cat food. Trying not to trip over the cats circling my legs like hungry sharks, I supervise as the boys dig into the cat food bin. They each jockey for the biggest scoop before dumping the dry food mostly into the bowls. Pressed for time, I make my way downstairs, grab pop-tarts from the cupboard, and hand them to the boys as they run past me. Despite my instructions not to make a mess, pop-tart pieces fly like shrapnel into the front seat before we've even pulled out of the garage.

Michael, now eleven and in the fourth grade, continues to attend the same private Christian school. Though we consider moving him to public school, pulling him away from his friends and routines seems cruel. Despite his tuition being nearly as much as our monthly mortgage, transportation to and from his school is not provided. Taylor attends first grade in a public school, but we live too close for bus service and too far for him to walk. So, I drive them both to school.

I chew on the tip of my fingernail while I wait for the light to change. From the backseat, I hear a sack lunch meet what I assume is a body part. Before a fight can break out, we pull into Michael's school. He hops out of the car. I struggle to keep my swearing to a minimum as the driver in front of me leans from her window to chitchat with another mom. Stay-at-home mothers seem to network continuously in the drop-off line. They make playdates, plan class parties, and organize fundraisers while I wait, trapped behind them with no way to get around. They irritate me. I tell myself I despise them for behaving as if they're the only people in the drop-off line, but really the reason is deeper. Although I work only part-time, I feel like an outsider in their world. I'm rarely up on school happenings. I'm not included in the purchasing of teachers' gifts, or organizing luncheons, or setting up fundraisers. I mostly don't attend their meetings, as they usually take place during my work hours. I know only a few of the parents outside of the school, and only because they attend our church. Whether intentional on their part or merely perceived on mine, I feel different from them. And I am different. I used to have sex with a woman and now I have sex with a man who isn't my husband. I'm bad, but I covertly take pleasure in the edginess it gives me. I plaster an irritated smile on my face and tap my fingers on the steering wheel. I consider saying something to the oblivious, blabbering mother, when a child's voice interrupts my thoughts.

"Jesus Christ, lady!" I peer into my rearview mirror and see Taylor roll his eyes. He exhales loudly over the sweatshirt sleeve wadded between his teeth, waves his free arm out the open window.

Any hope his outburst has gone unheard is dashed when I see the woman crane her neck around to glare at Taylor, and then me. I don't chastise him for his behavior, but rather I wait as the woman starts her car and drives away. The drop-off line at Taylor's school proceeds smoothly, and after a quick hug, my wee heathen jumps from the car and runs inside. I hear the vibration of my cell phone as I leave the school parking lot. I push the late library books off my phone, read the message as it fades.

"Meet me." A jolt of electricity shoots through my body.

Sex with Aaron has ramped up to the point that we are meeting whenever he can get away from work.

"Hey, babe, meet me at my house," Aaron's second message flashes across my screen.

My palms are wet, and they slip as I turn the steering wheel. I know the longer I put off answering, the less likely I'll say no. What do I even want with him? Not an orgasm; it's even more primal than that. I'm lured by the fury his touch ignites in me, the rage I, in turn, express free from repercussions: biting his tongue, calling him a bastard, or telling him to fuck off. This evil I must hide from the world, this wickedness that separates me from the other moms. I'm simultaneously disgusted and intrigued by the woman I am with Aaron. If Chet knew, ever found out, he would have every right to leave me, and still, I want Aaron.

I park up the street in front of a vacant lot where the neighbor usually keeps his trailer. I walk in the direction of Aaron's house, but avoid going to the front door. I sneak in through the garage entrance and his arms wrap around me before my eyes adjust to the dim light. His mouth covers mine; he smells of coffee. For a split second, I'm in the arms of someone else. I taste the rich flavor of coffee on Robin's tongue and hear her whispering my name in my ear as my feet leave the ground. But it's Aaron who carries me into his house, lays me out on the kitchen table. A child's plastic bowl clatters to the floor as Aaron climbs over a chair with a booster seat strapped to it. He balances above me on his forearms. We don't waste time removing our clothes but rather tug and pull fabric out of the way. He bangs me on the table, I feel a curl of flesh under my nail as I scrape his back with my nails.

"Careful," he yelps. "I don't want to have to explain any marks."

Instantly, I'm reeling back to earth and crashing head on into the present. "Get the fuck off!" I shove him away and clamber off the table.

My foot lands on the upturned plastic bowl and I lose my balance, but before I hit the floor, Aaron catches me.

"You okay?"

I shrug him away. He huffs, throws his hands up, and lets me find my own way out.

On the short drive home, my chest grows tighter and tighter, as if being squeezed by a blood pressure cuff. I concentrate on breathing, on pushing all thoughts from head. The only way to survive is to pretend nothing has happened. But something has happened, is happening. Cracks are forming beneath the surface of my resolve, stinging like a cut on my fingertip, and I'm struggling to keep my dual life separated.

I pull into the garage; the door closes automatically behind me. Inside the car, surrounded by silence, I shut my eyes and lean my head into the steering wheel. From behind my closed lids, Robin's image reappears, as comforting as a child's blanket. I trace the curve of her spine, feel the rough texture of her hair against my cheek, the softness of her lips on mine. I drift away, lulled by the sound of her voice. At the sudden blast of the car horn, I jerk my head up from the steering wheel and it falls silent. Not until I'm inside the house scrubbing dried food from the previous night's dishes do I notice the tears running down my cheeks. This must be the last time with Aaron. It must.

twelve

The following morning, I awake as if from a horrendous dream and am struck again with the memory of my sin. From there, I imagine the worst. I picture Chet discovering Aaron and me, the two men physically fighting, Chet telling all our family, friends, and whomever will listen about his slutty, cheating wife. Chet divorces me, takes away the kids, and I'm shunned by my entire family. I lose my house, my job, my car, I'm poor. In conclusion, I have to be done with Aaron.

I avoid running with him for a few days after texting him that I have a cold. When finally we do run again, conveniently, I've developed a stuffy nose. I show up each morning with a throat lozenge in my mouth to further sell the sick story. But I can only have a cold for so long, and three weeks later, I find myself brushing pine needles from my running tights. I straighten my clothes, stretch my neck, ready to run on. But Aaron doesn't move. His jaw is set. He's angry, which is peculiar, as I've just given him a blow job, which always puts him in a particularly good mood.

"Who else are you seeing?" he asks, not a hint of a smile on his face.

He can't be serious.

"I saw you," he snaps, "talking to that guy in the gym. You had your head tilted and you were practically fucking him with your eyes."

Oh my God, he is serious.

"What are you talking about?" I ask.

"I told you I didn't want you to see anyone else." He spits on the ground and takes off jogging.

I catch up to him, feel the anger bubbling up inside as I maneuver in front of him.

"I don't even know who you're talking about!"

"Whatever." He pushes me out of the way, runs ahead.

I let him go. I don't try to catch up to him again. He's being ridiculous, obviously offended I've avoided him the past couple of weeks. But I don't have time to argue, so I jog back home.

After dropping the kids at school, I drive to the gym. I'm not scheduled to teach classes or train clients, so I decide to lift weights and clear my head. I need a reset. I've never argued with Aaron before, and I don't know what to do with my feelings, because I don't even want to have feelings about him. That was the point: we fuck, we run, we text, and that's all—easy, uncomplicated. His tantrum is the last thing I need.

At the gym, I shove my bag into an empty locker. Out on the main floor, I head to the weights section. Picking up a set of hand weights, I position myself in front of the mirrors. From behind me, a guy with rabbit teeth is smiling at me. I realize he must be who Aaron is referring to. His name is Blake, and he's a regular at the gym, as well as a regular at Sunday church service. Since his recent divorce, he's taken a real interest in the gym—and me. Though I try to ignore him, he often attempts to make small talk.

"So, I'm thinking of hiring a trainer. You free?" Blake winks.

I cringe as I take in the chest hair vining in and out of the gold chain hanging from his neck. His back is against a weight machine and his feet are crossed casually at the ankles. He holds the ends of a white gym towel behind his head, grinning and flexing his biceps.

"Nothing is free," I reply, unsmiling.

Blake clears his throat, takes a step closer. He's bent so close to my ear his breath heats my skin. "*Train* me, Lorinda. Or do you only like certain guys?" He blows the question into my ear.

I'm taken aback by his brazenness and I step away from him, glancing nervously over my shoulder.

"I have to go to the bathroom," I mumble, and drop my hand weights to the floor.

I leave him standing alone as I beeline for the women's locker room. I lock myself into a stall and sit down on top of the toilet lid. I feel my pulse beating out a warning signal in my temple. I lean forward with my arms wrapped around my stomach and picture Aaron's accusing eyes and the way he tore off as if I hadn't just been on my knees with his dick in my mouth. Of course, he got what he wanted first. My eyes tear up as I realize what an idiot I am, what an idiot Aaron is! How can he think I'm seeing Blake? My cell phone buzzes in my pocket and I immediately hope to see a message from Aaron. I brighten when I recognize his number.

"I'm taking you out of my phone," his text reads.

I slap my hand over my mouth to stifle a cry. My hands feel numb as I stuff my phone back into my pocket. I stand, take a deep breath, and push open the stall door. I collect my things from my locker and walk out onto the gym floor. Blake is perched at the end of a weight bench a few feet from the entrance of the women's locker room. His bag is slung over his shoulder. I scan the gym floor again for onlookers, then saunter casually over to where he sits.

"So, where do you want me to train you?" I ask, tilting my head to the side until my hair falls over one eye.

He grins back, stands, and motions with his head for me to follow him. Even as I trail him, my conscience attempts to stop me. *Go home. Don't do this.* But I ignore the warning voice. It's too late, I need what he's got. I toss everything except my cell phone and keys into the backseat, lock up my car, and wait. Blake pulls alongside me in his black BMW. I look around one final time before I duck into his front seat. Usually hard-pressed to find my way out of a paper bag, as Blake drives, I attempt to make a mental note of both major and minor landmarks as we pass them. Just in case I should need to know and find my way back. We take the exit after Fred Meyer, and a private school and the Elks Lodge are the last buildings I see before Blake drives us out of town. Around the lake, fir trees, heavy under the burden of their branches, line the road on both sides. In the light breeze, they sway side to side, allowing an occasional peek at the rooftops hidden behind their otherwise impenetrable barrier.

As we drive, the sun hides behind a dollop of frothy white clouds just long enough to send a chill through my body. *What the hell am I doing?* I press my nose like an anxious puppy against the passenger window. But my apprehension lessens as the sun shines through again. Blake stops at a gate that stretches across the road. He keys in his pass code, disrupting the silence of our journey for the first time. The gate swings wide and we slowly drove through. The garage door is already opening as we crest the steep driveway. We pull inside and he kills the engine. I follow him up the steps into his mudroom, kick my shoes off next to his, the slate floor bites at the bottoms of my feet. A dog barks from the kitchen.

"That's Russ," Blake says.

Russ lifts his head and gazes at me through one open eye. My cold feet turn suddenly toasty, and I look to Blake for an answer to my unasked question.

"Heated floors," he says.

I squint at him in disbelief, then bend down and touch the floor with my palms. Heat radiates through the floor, warming my skin. I can't help but shake my head in wonder, I've never heard of such a thing. I stand and Blake wraps his arms around me.

"So much to teach you." He pulls me in for a kiss.

I reach under his shirt and rake my nails down the bare skin of his back. He laughs, grabs me around the waist. We slide along the wooden floor through his dining room, past a massive fireplace, then climb the stairs to his bedroom. At the end of the hall, Blake pushes open a door and leads me inside. My eyes widen and I halt in place. I cannot believe I am in the same house. The air is thick with dust, and the waning scent of overly dried flowers. Weary green and mauve floral drapes hang from the only window in the room, and a duvet of the same color and pattern lay spread across the bed. A wooden picture frame etched with the word "Forever" sits empty on the nightstand alongside a crystal vase filled with web-covered eucalyptus sprigs. I'm transfixed, frozen by the sudden change in aesthetics.

Blake reaches out his hand, leads me to the bed. I let him direct me back onto the mattress, feel my nipples harden as he runs his hands down my chest. He pulls my shirt over my head, then pulls off his own. I loop my fingers around the buttons of his jeans and pull. They pop open in succession without hesitation. Tucking my knees into my chest, I use my toes to grab at his pants, his briefs, yanking them down to his ankles. He closes his eyes as I scoot on my back, traveling to the spot between his legs. I hear him moan when I close my lips around his cock and commence to bob my head up and down. I'm functioning wholly on my junkie brain and scorching desire. So completely lost, so swept up in my mission that when suddenly Blake jerks his penis out of my mouth I yell, "What the fuck?"

"I don't want to do this," he says. "I invited you here because I want to help you," Blake's voice falters with emotion.

I wrap my arms around my chest and scramble off the bed. I retrieve my shirt from the floor, put it on, and tuck it into my jeans.

"I'm sorry," he whispers, and suddenly, like a festering boil snagged by a rough touch, my anger splits wide open and I let it ooze all over him.

"Whoever gave you the idea that I need help?"

"God did, Lorinda. I've been praying for you and God told me to intervene."

Intervene?

"I know about you," he continues, "I can help you. We can help each other."

What is he talking about? "Blake, I don't know what you want from me, but I want you to take me back to the gym." I keep my voice calm, but steely.

"I'm not going to hurt you," he says. "I just want to be with you. To pray with you. We can support each other without having sex."

He reaches out his hand, takes mine, and pulls me toward him. "I understand what you're going through. We are the same."

I laugh nervously, try to take a step back. "I don't know what you're talking ab—" I begin, but Blake slaps his other hand over my lips. My head snaps back.

"Yes. You. Do," he growls through clenched teeth. "You're a sex addict just like I am."

Sirens blare in my head, my mouth fills with bile, and I lunge for the waste can. There are only two possibilities, either Blake is an angel sent from God to help me as he claims, or he's a serial murderer. Blake kneels beside me, pulls my hair from my face, recites scripture as if preaching from a pulpit. I spit into the waste basket.

"Flee from sexual immorality," he commands, tugging at my hair for emphasis. "All other sins a person commits are outside the body, but whoever sins sexually, sins against their own body."

His voice cuts sharply through the fog in my brain and I force myself to sit back on my heels. Blake pulls me into his chest and strokes my head. The chain around his neck catches my hair and rips a few strands from my scalp. I'm not sure what to do next. Messenger of God, or psychopath? I hold my breath, wait for him to make a move.

"I'll take you back." He lets me go.

I follow him to his car, sit rigidly in the passenger's seat. He gets in, takes my hand, and his fingers close gently around mine. As we drive, I feel the car picking up speed. My free hand grips the door handle as he takes the curves around the lake too fast. I turn only my eyes to look at him. His gaze is fixed on the road ahead and the warmth in his touch has disappeared. Demons seem to crowd his conscience, and he drives as if he can't be rid of me fast enough, as if to shake me off like a poorly made decision. The Elks Lodge and the little private school with its brightly colored playground toys whip past in a blur. We leave the freeway, take the exit before Fred Meyer onto the road leading back to the gym. Blake squeals his tires as he pulls into the gym parking lot, barely rolling to a stop before he reaches across my body, pushes the door open, and shoves me out.

My legs are unsteady as I walk to my car. I climb in, lock the doors, and lean back in my seat. What just happened? What the fuck just happened? I wait for my heart rate to slow. I close my eyes. *Breathe, breathe, breathe.*

thirteen

The following evening, Chet and I sit with our feet kicked up on the coffee table. We've finally got the kids to bed and popped the latest blockbuster superhero movie into the DVD player. I lean on Chet's shoulder. He doesn't move to embrace me. His body feels hard, unyielding. My phone vibrates. In the few seconds it takes for me to realize it's ringing, Chet has it in his hand and is reading the partial message displayed across the screen.

"Hey, wanna meet?"

I snatch the phone from his hand.

"Who wants to meet you?"

I sink back into the couch and bring up the message. It's from Aaron, and my heart leaps.

"A friend from the gym wanting to meet for a run." I shrug my shoulders, return my eyes to the movie we're watching.

The reassurance I feel at having Aaron back makes me momentarily giddy. Then I hear Blake's words, feel Chet's shoulder against mine, and my worlds collide.

Maybe I am like Blake, a sex addict. I must stop having sex with Aaron. I definitely won't see that whack job, Blake, again. I *will* break through the wall between Chet and me and I *will* start over.

Blake accusing me of being a sex addict, declaring God told him to save me, is enough to give me a serious case of the creeps. I'm alarmed enough to turn down running offers from Aaron. At the gym, I focus solely on teaching my classes and training my clients, then head directly home. And at home, I occupy every available minute scrubbing the bathrooms, vacuuming twice a day, and even organizing Chet's tools in the garage. I must. The busier I am, the less chance I have of getting into trouble. Idle hands are the devil's workshop.

As the days and weeks add up, I remain faithful to Chet and mentally pat myself on the back. Of course, not cheating is not enough. I need to initiate intimacy with him, so he'll believe I sexually desire him. I should; I'm his wife and there's nothing I find physically unattractive about him. He has a beautiful muscular build, perfectly proportioned. I joke he would make an ideal specimen for an underwear model. His skin is light tan, naturally smooth, and his blue eyes get lost between his thick, feathery eyelashes. He can be witty and charming. I do love him. The issue is the way I love him. On one hand, I have a maternal compulsion to protect him, and on the other, I want him to take care of me. I adore being wrapped inside his powerful arms, protected from the world outside, but I don't want to have sex. I lecture myself on my marital duties as his wife. I pray. I pray more. I remind myself there are worse things than having sex with my husband, but the only way I can even become aroused, though I know it's sinful, is imagining Robin. I envision being enveloped by her fingers, her tongue, her smell, and this creates in me an erotic enough reaction, I can perform for Chet. The more frequently I summon these images, the quicker they materialize, becoming second nature. Still, this doesn't prevent me from being guilted by bits of Bible verses flashing like warning signs in my mind that even looking at another lustfully is committing adultery in the heart. I reason the verses apply to straight marriages, and because I'm not visualizing other men, this is a lesser sin. And anyway, what other choice do I have? I can't tell anyone how I really feel, and even if I did, what could be done? I am a Christian, a wife. I must be straight, or at the very least, straight enough.

One morning, after returning home from shuttling the kids to school, I run up the steps to our bathroom. I dim the vanity lights and peel off my clothes. My heart ticks faster with each piece of clothing I remove. I pose fully naked in front of the mirror. My breasts are too small, and since babies, too flat. I've never had a flat belly, but now I have stretch marks etched into my pale skin. *Ugh.* I take a deep breath, angle my cell phone camera, and click. I loathe seeing myself naked, but I send the photo to Chet anyway. He responds immediately.

"Hell yeah!" he texts, followed by a row of smiley emojis.

I close my phone, face the mirror. I comb out my long hair, letting it fall around my shoulders the way Chet likes it. I carefully paint liner under each eye, pat my eyelids with shimmering shadow, and coat my lashes with thickening mascara. My dresser drawer is stuffed with sexy underwear, lacy bras, and camisoles that I seldom wear; there's absolutely nothing redeeming about thong underwear. I grab the flimsy bit of silk anyway and step into it. Maybe if I wear it all day, I'll get used to it. But immediately I'm digging it out of my crack. I hook the matching bra around my chest and find my tightest jeans. My low-cut T-shirt is low enough that a hint of lace from my bra is visible. I wink at my reflection. Chet will think of nothing else the rest of the day, and I'll be ready. I've got this, I'm on a roll now, I ignore the niggling question in the back of my mind, but for how long?

When Chet walks through the door that evening and grabs me from behind, I return his flirtatious advance with giggles rather than slapping his hands away. I speed dinner along and prompt the kids to get to bed on time. By the time I'm finished, Chet's already naked and waiting for me in bed. I slide between the sheets and barely have a chance to wiggle out of my sexy underwear before he's on me. Heat radiates from his body and his sweat drips down my stomach. Our wet bodies slipping against one another grosses me out, but I push away my discomfort. Instead, I focus on my fantasy of being with Robin. I will Chet's body to morph into Robin's body. When he pushes inside of me, I feel Robin's fingers spreading. But when Chet tries to kiss my lips, I turn away. His kiss lands on my cheek. Jolted from my dream, I struggle to return my thoughts to Robin, but she's gone. Chet continues to move, to finish. When finally he spasms, gasps, and rolls off me, I steal a glance at his face. His mouth is set in a line, his eyes cold, he's pissed. Wordlessly, we turn away from each other, retreat to our separate sides of the bed. I listen as he begins to snore. There is a weight in my gut. Like all the progress I've made with Chet has been wiped away. I couldn't even pretend to enjoy having sex with him. I know I don't deserve Chet. I also know I can't live like this.

The next week at therapy, the Beller peers at me from behind her reading glasses, rocks back and forth. I notice the grooves worn into the floorboards beneath her chair and wonder how many of those indentions have been made during sessions with me. I rub my knuckles against my forehead. Why am I even here? Why do I think she can help, that anyone can?

"Tell me what's going on, Lorinda."

I shift on the leather couch, pull my legs up under me, try to get comfortable. My nerves send chills through my body, so I grab the aqua afghan tucked into the corner of the couch and wrap it around my shoulders. The Beller is waiting. I drop my feet back to the ground, clear my throat. She pulls her glasses off, ceases rocking.

"Have you started to see Aaron again?"

My face burns with shame, my mind wanders back to the events leading up to my reuniting with Aaron. Back to falling out with Chet, again.

Chet quit trying with me again, basically ignoring me after I ruined our special night. He intended on making a point. He wanted me to know he was upset; it was my fault, and I would have to pay. What he didn't know, couldn't know, was how severely I punished myself. If I could carve the evil out of me, I would. I felt the weight of my failure every day, I saw it in Chet's resigned expression and in the trusting blue eyes of my children.

Aaron texted me, and after I'd spent weeks wallowing in my disgrace, I responded. We met in the woods between our houses. He didn't apologize for our spat and I didn't bring it up. He'd been drinking, I smelled alcohol on his breath. He pulled me behind a tree, covered my mouth with his. Without a semblance of grace, we wrestled to the ground. I pulled his dick out of his jeans and he lifted my skirt. He thrust inside of me, his eyes glazed. I turned my head away, but he didn't care. He rammed into me over and over until I could feel I'd scooted too close to the tree trunk. My head smacked against the rough bark, but I didn't stop him. He didn't have a condom but was at least coherent enough to pull out. He crammed his cock in my mouth. I let my throat slacken, then swallowed, managing not to gag. He stood, pulled his pants up, helped me to my feet. I brushed the pine needles from my knees. We didn't have to talk. I didn't have anything to say anyway. I was high, floating miles away from and above my failings, from my glaring inadequacies.

"Lorinda." The Beller looks intently into my eyes as if to coax words from my larynx, but my throat constricts around impending tears. I don't *see* Aaron, I *fuck* Aaron. I'm a fucking whore. I stare at the clipboard she is holding, but don't reach for it, I'm not willing to commit my thoughts to paper today. I loop my fingers through the afghan, weave them in and out of the rows of geometric designs. I squeeze my hands into fists, hold the crocheted yarn as tightly as I can, desperate for something to cling to.

"Have you thought that maybe you would rather be with women?"

Not this again.

The Beller lays the clipboard on my lap. "Being gay is not an illness, Lorinda. It's not a sin."

I mentally kick myself for the millionth time for telling her about Robin. She's so hung up on her that she fails to see my real issues. I unravel my fingers, pick up the clipboard and pen.

"I'm not interested in women. I want to be sexually attracted to Chet. I want to stop sleeping with other men." I shove the clipboard back into The Beller's hands.

She reads my answer. She opens, then closes, her mouth. The Beller and I have been together off and on, sometimes more on, other times more off, for nearly eight years. At this point I describe our relationship as balancing precariously on what we each perceive to be the truth. My deep-seated truth being evangelical, Christian hierarchy, unattainable goals, and constant fear. The Beller, higher education and a Zen-like approach to live and let live. Continuing to see her instead of one of the recommended therapists from my church is significant, and doesn't go unnoticed by the Beller. She pulls her shawl like two crocheted wings around her shoulders as she leans back in her rocking chair.

"So, you're not attracted to women?" she clarifies, "and you *want* to be with your husband?"

I nod. She's a fucking broken record.

"Couples' counseling could be helpful," she suggests.

I stare at her. Couples' counseling? How can I explain to Chet the need for couples' counseling when he has no idea what's even going on? I sigh. I'm not ready to abandon the hope of becoming a faithful, straight, Christian wife, but I can't ask Chet to do counseling, and I'm just too tired to try to explain my reasons to The

Beller. But if not her, then whom? Whom do I turn to with my horrendous, adulteress behavior and seek help? There's no one, I know no one. Then, like a miracle straight from God himself, I receive my answer.

The following Sunday, as I sit next to Chet in church half listening, half planning what to make for lunch when we get home, I hear the pastor say, ". . . Living Waters is a program that will take place on Mondays for the next nine months in the old sanctuary. This program is suitable for our brothers and sisters dealing with unwanted same-sex attraction, victims of sexual abuse, and really all those who are experiencing sexual brokenness. If you would like more information, you can call the number on the back of today's bulletin." I'm too embarrassed to turn the bulletin over, lest I should be spotted doing so. I wait until the congregation is called to prayer, and then I flip it over. There are groups for moms of preschoolers, grief groups, singles groups, and, at the very bottom, printed just above the needs of the local food bank: Living Waters, a group for the sexually broken. I rub my finger over the phone number. This is my answer.

The next morning, after Chet leaves for work and I've deposited the kids at school, I lace up my running shoes. There's a three-mile loop that won't take me any time at all, and then I'll drive myself directly to church to sign up for Living Waters.

As I run, I inhale deep breaths of crisp air, jump purposely on fallen orange and yellow leaves. Fall is my favorite time of year, and today I feel hopeful for the first time in a long time. God has answered my prayer and I know exactly what step I need to take next. I feel free. A smile spreads over my face as I leap and bound along. This is how I want to live, unencumbered by obligations to men I don't need or want in my life. Why have I lived like a captive for so long? My pocket vibrates. I'm happily too preoccupied to answer. The trail is busier this time of day. I'm forced to dodge between walkers, dogs, and jogging strollers. My phone vibrates again. I ignore it. I notice the dense expanse of trees as they sway along the borders of the trail, take pleasure in the crunch of the leaves under my hot pink running shoes, and vault over roots and rocks in my path. When I crest the first hill, I slow at the top to gaze down at the view of the city below. From here I can see downtown to the Herald building. Home to our local newspaper, it towers high above the other buildings. If I continue down this trail, it will eventually lead me to Whatcom Falls, the same falls I've been drawn to my whole life. I won't have time to run all the way there today. But I allow myself to visualize the crash of the water as it leaps off the cliffs and merges into the lake below. I imagine the feel of the water's spray as it peppers my face, mixing with my perspiration. My cell phone buzzes again, spoiling my daydream. I pull it from my pocket, fumble for the power button. I catch a glimpse of a partial message from Blake.

"Have you been tested for . . ." the message fades. But instead of opening the full message, I shake my head and slip my phone back into my pocket. Talking to Blake would only disrupt my serenity. Besides, he's in the past with Aaron and I'm on the path to healing now. Or, this is what I tell myself, but I'm not quite able to completely squelch my curiosity. I flip the phone open.

"Have you been tested for STDs? For AIDS?" I swipe the sweat from my forehead, read it again.

What the fuck?

"No." I punch in before zipping the phone back into my jacket pocket. I try to focus on my breathing, on the sound of my feet hitting the ground. Why would I need to be tested? We didn't even have sex. When the vibration against my ribcage becomes constant, I realize my phone is ringing. I press it to my ear, managing only a partial hello before Blake's frantic voice drowns out mine.

"How can you be sure?"

"I just *am*." I'm not sure, but if I do have AIDS, it's not because of him.

"I want you to get tested. It's the only way I'll be able to let it go."

He's near hysteria, making my temple throb. Anger is building in the pit of my stomach.

"Why don't *you* get tested!" I hold down the power button until the screen goes black.

I turn around on the trail. I'm annoyed, thrown off, I may as well just go back home and shower. The path gives way to the paved cul-de-sac where my house sits between two others. I spot Blake pacing back and forth in front of his BMW, parked police-barrier-style across my driveway. Goosebumps pop up along my arms. I divert my eyes and run up the porch stairs.

"You shouldn't be here," I say, as much to myself as to him.

He takes the front porch steps two at a time and is right behind me as I fumble with the door lock.

"I'll take you to the clinic," he insists.

His hand closes tightly around my shoulder, my keys slip from my hands. I'm trembling as I reach to pick them up. Blake maintains a firm hold on my shoulder.

"Get. In. The. Car."

Too afraid to resist, to make a scene in my own neighborhood, I follow him to his car and reluctantly climb in. He tells me there's a clinic downtown that tests without appointments; he's obviously done his research. He has the exact amount of cash required, and hands it over without question to the woman behind the counter. She, in turn, hands him a clipboard with several forms attached and a pen sprouting limp fabric daisies. With his hand in the small of my back, Blake leads me to a chair in the corner of the room. He hands me the clipboard and pen, practically leans into my lap.

"Use my address and phone number." He's so close I feel like elbowing him.

"You want the test; you fill out the papers." I drop the pen and clipboard in his lap, lean my head against the wall.

My stomach knots as I picture a needle the length of my arm. A nurse approaches wearing pink scrubs raining cats and dogs. She calls my name and I follow her down the hall. She directs me to an examination room, points to a chair. I sit and she assures me the test will be quick. I look away as the tubes fill with my blood. The nurse smiles and holds a cotton ball over the needle prick as she secures it with tape.

"The AIDS results will be mailed to the address you've provided," she says as if having an AIDS test is the most common thing in the world.

But I know that homosexuals get AIDS, not married Christian women. I try to focus on her words, but I've already lost my footing and I'm floating away from her, from her words, from the room. When I return to the waiting room, Blake stands and reaches for my arm. I'm too dazed to resist, so I let him guide me out of the clinic and back to his car. He opens the passenger door, waits patiently for me to settle in. I wrap my arms tightly around my body. I feel small and completely empty. The weight of Blake's stare makes me turn toward him and I catch the fading smile as it leaves his lips. Instead of returning me home, Blake drives us to an empty construction site we'd passed on our way to the clinic. He pulls the car behind an overflowing dumpster and shifts into park. I'm numb from the clinic experience, and at the same time, enraged. I close my eyes as Blake's fingers roughly lift my chin. His kiss is angry, almost cruel in its harshness. His teeth scrape painfully along my lip. I taste my blood on my tongue. I open my eyes, see him wipe his hand across his mouth, inspect it for blood. I feel a physical change in my character, a hardening, and I lick my lips. *Well now you might get my AIDS.* I lunge at Blake, cover his mouth with mine. His hand snakes up the back of my shirt and unclasps my bra. My breasts fall free against my skin, I feel the familiar rush in my chest. Blake's breath is ragged in my ear. He doesn't stop me as I move down on him and take him in my mouth. My plan to join Living Waters has all but faded away. Here, with Blake, I'm an addict, we're addicts, violently addicted, and I no longer care about being healed.

fourteen

Once home, I walk numbly into the shower. As soon as the water hits, I scrub my skin until it hurts from the friction. The water temperature is as hot as I can stand; still, I smell Blake. My tongue burns from holding Listerine in my mouth; still, I taste him. Why do I do this? I watch as the water swirls down the drain, if only I could wash away my infidelity as easily. I dress and make some coffee to take along.

The little blue house sits directly across the street from my church and is not unlike the other houses on the block. The yard is neatly trimmed, encircled by a white picket fence. Planter boxes brim with fall foliage and the red front door frames a welcome sign painted in shapely black cursive letters. The sign smacks an alert against the door as I push it open. A woman, hair coiled in a bun held by a pencil, looks up from behind her desk. I'm immediately captivated. With her perfectly shaped lips, flawless skin, and defined cheekbones, she's gorgeous.

"Hello," she smiles, "I'm Dawn, and you must be Lorinda?"

I nod, take a step closer to her desk.

"Welcome. I have just a bit of paperwork for you to fill out." She points to a stack of forms piled neatly on her desk. I nod again.

I run my tongue along the inside of my lip, wince at the tender spot left by Blake. I force myself to pick up the pile of papers. Dawn hands me a pencil. I sit down in a corner of the room and prop the paperwork on the chair arm. A tentacle from a vining plant perched on a bookcase above me weaves through the open shelving. It crawls down the wall, dangling less than an inch above my head, grabbing at wisps of my hair as if to hold me in place. I instinctively lean away, roll my shoulders a couple of times, and take a deep breath. I skim over the documents. Along the top of each page is a question, followed by several blank lines. Well, at least writing is something I can do.

The first question dives right in, and I realize there will be no dodging the issues at hand.

How do you define your relational, emotional, or sexual problems (same-sex attraction, addictive behaviors, sexual promiscuity) and what impact, if any, do they have on your marriage?

Where's the Beller when I need her? I don't even know where to begin or what to include or omit. My knee bounces nervously, I close my eyes and try to visualize where to start. Without difficulty, I can recall the rough calluses on my uncle's palm as he brushed the hair from my neck and whispered, "You're my favorite." Is this what I should be writing? Are these the answers they're looking for? If I write about him, do I write about Robin?

And the girl from sixth grade? I flip the page, maybe the next question will be easier.

How does the problem express itself? (include compulsive non-sexual behaviors)

I'm recently aware that compulsive behavior is a coping mechanism. The Beller tells me that millions of people suffer from at least one compulsive behavior. That these behaviors are actions engaged in repeatedly, even when an individual wishes they could stop, even though they trigger negative outcomes, lead to interpersonal conflicts, or damage mental health. There are many common activities that can develop into compulsions, like shopping, hoarding, eating, gambling, sex, and exercise. Of course, these behaviors rarely decrease anxiety in the long run; in most cases, they only provide temporary relief. In extreme cases, compulsive behaviors start to take over a person's work, home, and social life, at the expense of normal activities. She suggests my issues with cleaning, exercise, and especially sex could be viewed as compulsive behavior, which she assures me is understandable when a person feels out of control in so many other areas of his or her life. I do clean the entire house every day. Organizing the kids' toys, picking them up the moment they leave them unattended. I face bottles, cans, anything with words, labels forward, and I do two or three loads of laundry every day. Even if I don't feel well, I still clean my house. If I host a gathering or party, I can think only of the cleaning I'll do once everyone is gone. This fixation on cleaning ties for first place only with my obsession for exercising. I never miss a workout unless I am too sick. I fall into bed at night hungry, and often dream I've gorged on junk food. When I awake, I immediately press my fingers into my ribs to be sure I haven't. If I do eat too much, I throw up because I cannot bear the thought of what will happen if I don't. I hate my body. I avoid looking at myself naked because I only see the pot belly, dimply thighs, and saggy breasts; I find this infuriating. I've wanted a flat stomach since the day Mom told me I needed to wear a one-piece bathing suit because I wasn't shaped for a bikini. I was eight years old, but I was already fat. As for excessive sex, well, *duh*. I'm a sex addict, though the Beller suggests antidepressants may help with this, too. Mental drugs are for those who are too weak to have faith in God, and I cannot add this to my already growing list of sinful failures.

Describe your moral position on sexuality, e.g., the parameters for sexual expression. Include your views on homosexual practice.

Obviously, I know the appropriate answer: homosexuality is wrong, sex outside of marriage is wrong, anything outside the husband-and-wife model held by the church is unacceptable. This truth is black-and-white, with absolutely no room for gray, and the primary reason I need Living Waters.

Have you ever been convicted of a felony? If yes, please explain.

Felony. They let in people who'd committed felonies.

"Here's a confidentiality and release of liability page for you to sign." Dawn has appeared in front of me. "Also, some books for you to purchase."

I scratch out my signature, hand over my finished forms.

"The first meeting is tonight in the old sanctuary." She hands me a stack of books. "Bring these."

I take them and exit the little blue house.

That night I have dinner laid out on the table when Chet walks in. Michael and Taylor bounce in their chairs, thrilled to have their playmate home. Chet tosses his lunch box on the counter and ruffles the boys' hair before he pulls back his chair. When Chet bows his head, the boys quiet and say a prayer of thanks for the meal.

"I have a meeting at the church tonight." I pour milk into Chet's glass.

"What kind of meeting?" His eyes seek mine as he butters his roll with more butter than could even be considered remotely healthy.

Built not unlike a professional athlete   not an ounce of visible fat—he never listens when I caution him on his eating habits. Instead, he gives me a wink while flexing and kisses his own bicep. It's hard to argue with someone who looks as fit as he does. With broad shoulders, visible abdominal muscles, and powerful legs, he's often mistaken for a bodybuilder, though he hasn't lifted a barbell in years.

"It's about intimacy stuff." I shift my eyes side to side, indicating the little ears listening.

He nods as he holds my gaze. The fact that I'm the one turning to the church for help is likely validating his belief that the sexual issues we face are solely mine. And aren't they? I cram the last few dishes into the dishwasher and notice Chet covering the leftovers and putting them into the fridge. Watching him as he rearranges and stacks containers, careful not to mess up the organization I work so hard to maintain, I feel a stab of sadness. He's just a regular guy who wants a regular life and a normal wife. Why can't I be her?

"So, is this Living Waters something we both need to attend?" Chet sounds genuinely interested, but the *last* thing I want is for him to be there.

Chet touches me gently on the cheek. I tense. I wipe my hands on my apron, shake my head.

"No, I need to do this myself. It's my problem, I need to work it out," I assure him.

He rests his hand on my shoulder, his expression serious. "Robin was older than you, she persuaded you. I hope this program will help you let go so we can move on." He kisses me on the forehead.

I'm taken back by his comment, but of course, he knows nothing of the other men, of my secret life. I feel even more certain I need forgiveness I can only find in the church community. I *need* Living Waters. I snag my coat and shoulder bag and head for the door. Chet and the boys yell goodbye as they run for the living room. They pile on top of one another on the floor, rolling around in a tangled ball of arms, legs, and delighted squeals of laughter.

At the church, I park in the back of the parking lot away from all the other cars. I glance around as I gather my stuff and head toward the building. I hope no one sees me, though few people likely mill around church on a Monday night. I walk through the doors of the old sanctuary and pull my coat a little tighter. Once used as the main building where Sunday services were held, over the years, a new, much larger sanctuary has been built to house the church's growing congregation. This old space has been repurposed as a meeting room. The windows on the doors are covered with black paper, and I wonder if that's to keep the light out or the evil in? Rows of folding chairs, an aisle down the middle, face the stage where a wooden cross looms from the center. I imagine Jesus hanging from the cross, adorned in white cloth, wearing a crown of thorns, and my heart is burdened with shame. The room fills with the sounds of shuffling feet and groaning chairs as people settle into seats. From where I sit, I realize Dawn is impressively tall, her hair now more neatly clipped behind her head, the pencil from this morning replaced with a decorative clasp. She speaks with authority, loud enough so as to not require a microphone, displaying the coolness of a runway model as she walks to center stage.

"Welcome to Living Waters." Dawn smiles, sweeps open her arms wide, as if intending to wrap us all in a maternal hug.

Some heads bob in greeting, others remain forward, eyes fixed ahead. She begins by providing us a brief history of the Living Waters program. Andrew Comiskey, the founder, formed the program in 1980 while serving as a staff member for the Vineyard Church in west Los Angeles. That same year, he married his wife, Annette, and they eventually had six children. Comiskey professes that through his relationship with God, he was able to leave behind the gay lifestyle and transform into a straight man. I flip over the required text and come face-to-face with Comiskey's piercing blue eyes and alluring grin. I note his slender frame, the way he holds his delicate hands clasped beneath his chin, and I imagine gay men everywhere disappointed at losing him to the other side. I turn the book back over and scan the pages for a photo of his wife, but don't find one. Comisky claims that Living Waters is not conversion therapy but rather a pathway to healing and restoration to sexual wholeness. He boasts that his program has grown beyond healing homosexuality to include healing for the sexually abused, as well as for addiction to pornography and sex addicts. I look around the room again. There are fit-looking younger men, older men with soft bellies and plenty in between. The women look to be nearly all middle age and above, and greatly outnumber the men. I recognize a few from weekly church services but am relieved to find that I don't know any of them by name. The history lesson concludes, and Dawn introduces her staff. There are five female and five male mentors. The men describe their addictions to sex, pornography, and masturbation, and how God has miraculously healed them, set them free to live the life he's intended for them. As they share personal details, I rub circles into my knuckles with my thumb. I'm uncomfortable hearing such intimate confessions spoken in a group setting and utterly recoil at the idea of doing the same. The first female mentor to speak claims she's been healed from the sin of homosexuality. Her name is Nina, and she is tall. Her athletic build and cropped, graying hair suggest she may be less runway model and more basketball player. When she speaks, her voice is unexpectedly tentative. I strain to hear as she describes her long-term relationship with a woman she willingly gave up five years earlier.

"I'm not currently in a relationship." She pauses, looks down at the floor, "I haven't been since . . ." her voice trails off. When she looks up again, her bright smile contradicts the pain I imagine I see in her eyes.

I'm forced to think of Robin, of the day I was forced to give her up. The day I turned my back and abandoned her. I wonder if she will ever forgive me.

"But I am completely fulfilled in my relationship with God," Nina finishes, lifting her hands to heaven as people nod and murmur "amen."

The other female mentors share varying stories of sexual abuse leading them to frigidity in their marriages or preventing them from marrying at all. Many have suffered with some form of eating disorder. The common theme being that though they continue to wrestle with their eating and weight issues, they believe their relationships with their husbands, boyfriends, and, most importantly, God, have improved upon completion of the Living Waters program. When the last person has left the stage, Dawn announces that we will spend the next hour in worship. A couple of men and women gather in the front with guitars and microphones. One flips on an overhead projector, arranges a sheet of music. Around me people sway, raise their arms in surrender, and sing along with the lyrics projected on the wall. Repeatedly, they warble, until words are nothing more than sounds, completely carried away in the spirit. I can't shake Nina's testimony. She claims to be fulfilled, and I wonder if that is the same as sexually whole. I wonder if I'll be able to find fulfillment in my relationship with God. Because—complete disclosure—I still miss Robin and fear in the deepest recesses of my heart that maybe she's the only one who can ever fill the empty space. Hearing Nina speak, it's hard to imagine that she doesn't feel the same loss for her longtime lover, but I want to believe her, I need to believe her.

We're given a brief intermission before we launch into the third and final hour. I barely have time to grab a cup of coffee before Dawn calls everyone's attention back to the front of the sanctuary. She announces we'll be breaking into small groups. Throughout the sanctuary, our small group mentors hold up signs with names of those in their groups. I spot my name; Nina is my mentor. I follow her to a corner of the sanctuary. I choose a seat, set my coffee cup carefully beneath me. A woman plops down next to me, round face glistening with a fine sheen of sweat. She wrestles with a heavy bag slung over her shoulder. The bag lands in her lap, her fleshy arm grazes my shoulder.

"Sorry," she puffs, scoots away from me.

Nina greets us with a warm smile, then instructs us to go around the circle, give our names and a short explanation as to what we hope to accomplish in the program. Sweat prickles my forehead, I rub nervously at my arms.

"I'll get things started." Nina shifts in her seat. "I'm Nina. I've been with the Living Waters program five years. I joined to deal with my unwanted same-sex attraction. I've been free from the bondage of homosexuality for five years now." She sounds more convincing this time around.

The woman next to Nina admits to dealing with feelings of unworthiness after suffering years of sexual abuse by her father. She's recently broken off her wedding engagement because she's terrified she won't be able to perform sexually with her husband. *Whoa!*

Nina thanks her for her courage and looks to the next woman. *Oh, no way am I going to be able to do this.* The next woman whispers, and I can't make out what she says before she rests her head on her fingertips. But Nina nods, thanks her, and moves on. The next woman giggles nervously as she rubs her hands together. She confides to searching for healing for her marriage. Her husband cheated on her, and though she knows she'd be within her right to leave him, she's totally forgiven him.

"He's sorry," she assures us, as she bobs her head. "He promises it was a one-time thing, and I think it was mostly the other woman's fault."

Shit. Next is a woman sitting with her back stiff against her chair, her lips pressed into a thin line. We remain quiet as we wait for her to speak, but she remains motionless. Finally, Nina leans slightly forward, "If you aren't ready to share, we can—"

"My husband molested our nieces and nephews and will probably go to prison. He's enrolled in the program, too," the woman blurts out.

A collective gasp rounds the circle. Nina simply nods and all eyes turn to me. My shirt feels clammy against my fleece jacket.

"I'm Lorinda." I rub my palms down my legs, hold onto my knees, will them to stop shaking. "I'm hoping for healing." My face burns hot and I'm too embarrassed to look around the circle, so I stare at my shoes.

"Is there a specific area in your life for which you are seeking healing?" Nina asks.

Oh, just a little problem I have with fucking men other than my husband. Oh, and then there was the one woman, too . . . I shake my head.

Without missing a beat, Nina thanks me and everyone for their openness and their bravery. But I don't feel brave, I feel weak. This was supposed to be where I laid it all out, came clean. I grasp the sides of the metal chair, bow my head in prayer with the others. Nina leaves the floor open to spontaneous prayers from the group, but we are silent. Eventually, she thanks the Lord for bringing us together and we all agree with a collective *amen.* Then, after giving us our assignments, Nina wishes us a blessed week ahead. I wonder if everyone will return the following week. I wonder if I will. This is my chance to get right with God and right with Chet. I *must* return, *must* make Living Waters work. I must leave my destructive behavior with other men behind me and move on. Chet deserves a faithful wife and I *want* to be faithful. My faithfulness will solve all of our problems. I open the sanctuary doors, slip quietly back into the real world.

fifteen

The Living Waters program is slated for nine months, and I hope—and, on some level, expect—it to completely fix me. After all, the program's been created by a homosexual man turned straight. What worthier evidence could I ask for? I already know how to feel and behave in the confines of my marriage, but I want my feelings to be authentic. So, I wait for God to work his miracle in me. Each Monday night, I listen to the featured speakers preach on topics as varied as the members I sit alongside— pedophiles, rapists, homosexuals, and those who masturbate. We're all the same, all sinners burdened with an innate corrupt nature, all descendants of Eve who tempted her God-fearing husband, Adam, with forbidden fruit, prompting the fall of mankind. As a result, our Living Waters mentors beseech us to submit our will to God's. For this is our only chance at salvation, our only hope for healing. In that vein, we share intimately our private thoughts, feelings, and fears in our small groups to remain accountable, one to another. I hear my mother's scolding voice in the back of my mind, "You know better." And she's right. I wish I could peel off my skin, flee my mind, my body, my life, but all I can do is vow to make Living Waters work. I must tear down my will and replace it with God's. I journal, pray, confess, and participate with conviction. I kneel in the sanctuary with my list of handwritten regrets, surrendering them at the foot of the cross. I swing a hammer, smashing to bits the brick representing my sinful bondage to adultery. I stand face-to-face with each person in Living Waters, even the felon, and say I forgive them as God has also forgiven me. In my real life, I tell Aaron we can't have sex anymore. I mean it. Every time I say it. And sometimes I last a month, maybe even two, before I relapse. I can't wholly blame Aaron, for I give in to him willingly, and afterward, giving in the next time becomes that much easier.

By 2010, I'm beginning my third year of Living Waters, and though I can't readily admit to it, I feel worse now than when I began. At least before Living Waters, when I fell off the straight and narrow into a rabbit hole of sinful despair, only I knew about it. Now I feel compelled to admit my transgressions to my small group, which, though meant to be comforting, is anything but. When I confess the ugly details of my sins, I can't help but imagine an oversized "A" blazing across my forehead. The other women in my group, though their faces change year to year, are the same. They're good women who've had bad things happen to them. They're seeking healing from pain inflicted on them, while I inflict pain on others and myself and I can't seem to stop.

I'm only a few weeks into year three when my small group mentor approaches me privately.

"I see you're back again. Well, don't be discouraged, you can still hear from the Lord, if you truly surrender to him."

I'm rattled by her words. Already insecure of my obvious incompetence at working the program, my anxiety continues to steadily build throughout the week. At first, I seek solace in frantically deep-cleaning my house. While I scrub toilets and showers and tear down clothes from my kids' closets, rehanging them in order by color, I pray God will infiltrate my evil heart, cleanse me of my sin and change my ways. A text message alert sounds, and I read Aaron wanting me to slip away with him. I delete the message without answering. I'm brushing mildew from the shower grout with a toothbrush when Aaron sends another text.

"Meet me for coffee."

Unlikely there will be any coffee involved.

I delete the message, toss my cell phone into my sock drawer, and head downstairs. I plunk a defrosted chicken into the crockpot, add some broth, and set it on low. I lean against the counter, drained. Maybe tonight I'll supplement dinner with pre-made side dishes, a luxury I rarely allow myself. I peek at the ticking clock hanging in the archway above my head. If I hurry, I'll have time to hit the grocery deli before collecting the kids from school. I sprint up the stairs to collect my cell phone from my sock drawer and then head for the store.

I swing into the parking lot, notice a black BMW parked and hogging up two spaces. *Asshole.* I search for and find a spot close to a cart return. I pop the trunk.

"Need some help?" A man's hand reaches over my head, pushes open the trunk a bit higher. I retrieve the reusable grocery bags and whip around to face Blake.

"What do you want?" I ask through clenched teeth.

Not waiting for a response, I stomp toward the store, but he catches up, steps in front of me.

"Move."

He remains in place.

I shift my weight from one leg to the other, throw up my hands. "What do you want?"

"Don't be angry. I was cleaning off my desk and found this." He holds out an envelope. "And I realized I never called you with the results."

I reach for the envelope, but he pulls it away, holds it over my head.

"So, I stuck it in my car in case I was lucky enough to run into you. And. Here. You. Are." He waves the envelope back and forth.

The black BMW, I mentally kick myself; I should have known it would be Blake. I stretch tall, balancing on my tiptoes and snatch the envelope from his hand. I hold my breath slightly as I survey the results.

Blake leans into my ear, brushes my hair away with his hand. "You're clean," he whispers.

I shrug him away, shove the envelope into my coat pocket. I leave him standing where he is and scoop up a basket from the stack inside the door. I turn to make sure he's gone and spot his BMW pulling away. No way running into Blake after all this time of never seeing him in the gym or anywhere else was coincidental. I'm thoroughly creeped out. I shake out my arms and legs like I did as a kid knocking off imaginary cooties.

With my basket swinging on my arm, I make my selections from the deli. Over the loudspeaker, a sales associate's announcement is a garbled message about a deal on hams or maybe yams. I turn into the produce section, sidestep a clump of indistinguishable squashed fruit on the floor. A man raps a cantaloupe with his knuckles, then holds the melon to his nose. I've never understood this way of deciphering whether a melon is ripe or not. His dark hair falls over his forehead, he shakes it out of his face. Plumelike lashes surround his dark eyes. He catches me staring. He winks. I turn away. Do I know him from the gym? Not that it matters, because I'm going to walk away, finish shopping, and head home. But I can't help stealing a quick glance over my shoulder. He's moved from cantaloupes to grapes. He picks up a bunch, inspects them before selecting them. His bicep flexes as he lifts his basket from the floor, transferring it from one hand to the other. By the time I've finished shopping and bring my groceries to checkout, he's made his way through the express lane and is leaving the store. I feel relieved. As if I've managed to avoid disaster, which is ridiculous because nothing was going to happen. The cashier hands me my receipt. I leave carrying my shopping bags in both arms, and spy winking produce guy leaned up against a tree in front of Starbucks. It's one of the skinny trees adorned in a knitted, multicolored sweater and scarf. Smoking in the shopping area is prohibited, but he's puffing a cigarette. Maybe I don't know him from the gym. He takes a long drag, tilts his chin to the sky, exhales slowly. Smoke swirls, dissipates, fades into the past. He tosses his cigarette down, grinds it into the dirt around the tree. When he spots me, his eyes crinkle around the edges, he winks again. Adrenaline courses through my veins, my head is swimming. I feel frantic, like time is running out. What I'm about to do will not erase the encounter with Blake, or fix my failure to reform in Living Waters, but in the end, my feet betray me anyway.

"Do I know you?" He slides his arm through mine.

I laugh, nod, let him lead me to his car. He takes my bags, tosses them into the back seat of his car, and locks the doors. I follow him as he walks to the very edge of the parking lot, behind the store, and down to the trail below. Aside from an elderly gentleman leading his equally elderly golden retriever by a leash, all is quiet. This is my trail. I know it by heart. Every twist and turn, every jutting rock and root along its path. I know where the vegetation thins, and house roofs become visible. I know where to go to disappear behind a heavy cover of trees, and that is where I lead him. The ground here is softer, covered by pine needles, but he runs his hand up my back and bends me forward. He pulls my pants down enough to drive himself inside me. He pulls my hair, slams me from behind, and in a matter of seconds, I feel him come. He flips me around, kisses me on the mouth. I shove him away hard, but he only laughs and zips his pants. My legs shake as I watch him stride away. His semen trickles down the inside of my thigh.

I'm nauseous as I slink back to my car. But as soon as I slide behind the steering wheel, I switch gears, begin mentally calculating the amount of time remaining until the kids are out of school. I pull into the garage, push open the kitchen door, set my keys on the counter. I pull down a stack of plates, arrange the table for dinner. The crockpot timer sounds, and I lift the lid. Steam from the browning chicken hits me in the face, and suddenly I remember the forgotten bags of groceries in the produce guy's car. I turn to the fridge to search for something else to serve, but as I scan the shelves, my vision blurs with tears.

Later, once the dinner dishes are cleared and the kids are tucked into bed, I can no longer deny my exhaustion. Cleaning house, avoiding Aaron all day, the encounter with Blake, and finally succumbing to the guy at the store, have totally consumed me. I have nothing left. Chet plays video games downstairs, but I head to bed. I slip between the covers, move into the middle of the bed. The sheets are cool against my skin. I spread my arms and legs out as far as they can go in the shape of an X. I exhale until my ribs stick out and all the air releases from my lungs. I close my eyes, inhale, and imagine Robin's warm hands running along my body as I drift to sleep. Minutes or hours later, I can't be sure, the sound of Chet grunting in my ear breaks the spell of sleep. I protest, attempt to roll away, but his legs on either side of my body pin me in place. I strive to float away outside of my reality, but instead I taste the saltiness of sweat dripping from his forehead as he holds me tight. When finally, he releases me, I feel a river running down my legs for the second time today. He rolls over, but I wait until I'm positive he's dropped off to sleep before I scoot away from him. I pull my knees into my chest, let the tears roll down my cheeks, and plead with God to help me. Living Waters isn't preventing me from fucking around, and whether it's my fault or theirs, I'm drowning.

sixteen

I am untouchable, unbreakable, dangerous. I fuck four guys, come home, fuck my husband, and make dinner. I sit next to women in church whose husbands I screw. I pray, I give head, I host Bible study, I bang in the woods, I bake cookies. I lie with a smile so unadulterated displayed across my face, my own mother doesn't suspect the evil lurking beneath. And I'm dying. This isn't the life I want. I want to be good. I want to be virtuous. I want to be honest. I want to be whole. But I'm failing. I'm failing at Living Waters, at being a wife, a mother, a person. So, if I'm not dying, I want to be. I want to be.

I work fifteen hours a week teaching at the gym and train a handful of clients, but with both kids in school full-time, I'm open to working more. So, when the library contacts me to ask if I'd like to fill in for a couple of days a week, I jump at the chance.

In the nearly ten years since leaving the library, little has changed. New books stack in precarious towers against the walls waiting to be cracked open and processed for delivery. The whir-ring of laminator fans, the snipping of scissors, and the hushed voices of library employees all meld together in a familiar hum. Before checking in with the department I'm to work in, I head to the delivery room. The desk once belonging to me is now sur-rounded by another employee's belongings—a lunch bag, a small, framed photo of a little girl, and an opened can of Coke. I don't want to appear too nosy, but when I catch a glimpse of a single remaining photo I tacked to the wall years earlier, I lean closer to get a better look. In the picture, I stand self-consciously in front of the library sign, squinting into the camera. Behind me, Robin peeks over my puffed-up '90s hair. The sound of her voice still rings in my ears, and I remember her whispering, "Hey, pretty lady, can I stand behind you?" I slide my finger under the photo, pull it free from the wall, let the tacks fall to the ground. I shove it into my pants pocket just as the delivery room door flings wide and the current delivery driver walks in. He stops abruptly when he sees me looking startled, and asks if he can help me. I shake my head as he takes his seat at Robin's desk. I feel a wave of sad-ness seeing him sitting there instead of her.

In the accounting department, at the computer desk provided to me, a sticky note next to the keyboard instructs me to log in to accounting. I do so with my old passwords and make a pit stop into my email. My inbox is jammed with absolutely nothing I'll ever need, but my OCD makes it impossible for me to ignore. Mostly mass email notices sent to all library employees updating policies, I only half scan the subject lines before moving them to the trash. But then my own name catches my eye and I stop. I unhighlight the chunk of mail I'm about to delete and click on the one that reads, "Hey, Lorinda, it's me," and open the email.

Howdy, darlin',
I'm not sure you will ever see this, but I thought I'd give it a shot. Here's my phone number: (208) 441-5778.
Love you,
Robin

My heart moves up my throat. I lean closer to the screen, read it again. I'm unable to pull my eyes away from the screen.

"Can you run this deposit to the treasurer's office, please?" The accountant holds a money bag in my direction.

I minimize the screen, take the bag from her. But when she returns to her desk, I maximize the screen, reread the email. I realize the date on the email is over two years old. I want to cry. But I rip a sticky note from the pad next to the computer and scribble down her number anyway.

On my way to the courthouse, I smooth out the sticky note on the empty seat next to me. Electricity runs through my arm each time I stroke the paper, the closest I've been to her in ten years. I pull into a spot in front of the courthouse and just sit for a moment. I stare at the Post-it, at her number, and eventually reach into my jacket pocket to feel for my cell phone.

Should I call? What if she doesn't answer? What if she does?

Finally, I tap her number, hold the phone to my ear. By the sixth ring, I give up hoping she'll answer. I don't bother to leave a message, and instead shove my phone into the glove box.

The courthouse is filled with a new round of jury duty victims. They file in like a row of unruly school children on a field trip. There's no easy way around them, so I wait. When I spot an opening in the line, I dart through, head to the treasurer's office. I push open the heavy wooden doors and take my place in the back of the line. I lean my weight onto one leg, stare down at the faded, diamond-patterned tile floor. Should I have left Robin a message?

"Next!" calls the woman from behind the counter. She leans heavily on her elbows, tapping out a staccato rhythm with the tip of her pencil.

I shove the money bag across the counter. She counts it, enters the deposit, hands me a handwritten receipt and the bag, and yells for the next customer. I barely have a chance to step away from the window before the next person in line slaps their deposit down on the counter. From the treasurer's office, I head back through the courthouse, which has cleared considerably. When I open the door to my car, I hear vibrating coming from the glovebox. I lunge across the passenger seat and rip open the glove box. I fumble around, trying to grab my phone before it quits ringing, and somehow, I manage to answer.

"Hello!" I yell too loudly, embarrassing myself.

I try to calm my breathing as I listen for a reply. But the phone's quiet. I've obviously missed whoever called. And then I hear her familiar drawl.

"Well, howdy, darlin'."

I feel swells of frantic laughter welling up inside of me until I laugh out loud, and then immediately, I begin to cry. I cry until I'm hiccupping. I apologize, but Robin only chuckles.

"Darlin', I'm so glad to hear from you."

I slow my breathing and my hiccupping lessens. I don't know what to ask first, so I bombard her with questions. She tells me that after leaving the library, she moved to Idaho with a woman she met in Bellingham. When that relationship didn't work out, she moved in with another woman in Ritzville, and even though that hasn't worked out either, she remains there with the woman and the animals they acquired together. I bristle as she casually speaks of other women.

"When I come to Bellingham to visit my family," she asks, "will you see me?"

My heart leaps. I've dreamed of this more times than I can remember, but now with Living Waters, seeing her is literally the last thing I should be considering. But I do, and there is no way I will tell her no.

"Certainly," I agree.

"I love you," she says. I feel my throat tighten.

"Me, too."

We hang up and I lean my head back against the car seat. Have I really spoken to Robin? I suddenly feel very warm. I roll the car window down and lean out into the cool air. I know I need to get back to the library, and yet I hate to move on with real life, to break the magic of this moment.

The rest of the afternoon, I play my conversation with Robin repeatedly in my head. I can't help obsessing at the possibility of seeing her again. When I close my eyes, I can imagine my elation at finally running into her arms after being separated for so many years. But then my guilty conscience shakes me violently back to the present. Back and forth, back and forth I struggle, until by the end of the week, I'm going stir-crazy.

"So, let's check in," chirps Nina in Living Waters on Monday night. "Lorinda, let's begin with you."

I cringe. I should come out with the truth, but I'm still trying to sort it out. I don't know how to explain how I'm feeling. I only ever mentioned Robin in the sign-up paperwork. In small group, I seek repentance for the men I've screwed. Am I ready to delve into this whole new can of worms? Year three and I just now bring up Robin?

"I'm doing really well." I rock back in my chair.

The usually silent, emaciated wisp of a woman seated to my right speaks up. "You don't *look* well." She's barely audible. I almost laugh aloud.

"In what way do you think Lorinda looks unwell?" Nina asks.

Oh my God, why is she going to entertain this woman? My face burns at being the center of attention. The woman uncurls her arms, pulls her feet up off the ground, and sits crisscross in her chair.

"She looks nervous. Like she's not telling the truth," she replies, twisting her arms.

Nina faces me. "Lorinda, how do you feel about what she's saying?"

A million thoughts race through my mind and not one is to tell the truth, and yet, that's exactly what I do.

"There is a woman . . ." I begin, unable to keep the quiver out of my voice.

Nina waits patiently. I shift in my chair, painfully aware that every eye in the group is locked on me. I must explain so they will understand she's not just *any* woman.

"What about the woman?" Nina questions, cautiously treating me as if I'm a frightened animal about to bolt.

Without giving myself a chance to chicken out, I go for it. "We were once involved," I begin. "I heard from her last week for the first time in ten years." Unable to hold myself together any longer, I break into tears. "And I love her," I choke out.

The group is silent. I can't look up and risk making eye contact with anyone. After what feels like an unreasonably long time, Nina rests her hand on my shoulder, instructs our group to hold hands.

"Let's bow our heads and listen for the Holy Spirit to speak."

My hands are clammy. Fingers close around mine and Nina implores the Holy Spirit for words of wisdom and direction. I pray along with her, fully expecting an answer. This is the night my prayers will be answered. This is what all the years and months of this program have been leading up to. Now that I've laid out my truth, my whole truth, I can be healed. My heart can be changed, and I can be made new. I hear murmurs of "praise be to God" and "your will be done," and finally, Nina closes us in a collective "amen."

I'm a bit let down when the group rises to pick up and fold their chairs. I hoped for clarity at the very least about what my next move should be, but I don't actually feel anything. I place my chair carefully along the wall with the others and notice Nina on the other side of the room talking with Dawn. I button my jacket.

"Lorinda, can you stay behind for a few minutes?" calls Dawn. "We'd like to talk to you in private."

Nina flashes a limp smile; I feel the prickling of sweat under my fleece vest. When the last person exits the sanctuary, Dawn motions for me to sit down on the steps of the stage between her and Nina. Dawn holds a clipboard and pen on her lap.

"Lorinda, I hope by now you know how loved you are by all of us and by your heavenly father." I look to Nina, she remains silent.

"As a way of maintaining healthy boundaries and ensuring this program continues to provide a safe healing place for you and everyone, I'd like you to read and sign this contract." She holds out the clipboard. I take it, read the first line to myself.

I _____ will abstain from contacting persons of the same sex for the purpose of sexual relations, or physically intimate relationships of any kind beginning this day _____.

I read it again. My eyes boomerang back to the word "abstain." I repeat the word aloud. "Abstain."

And for the first time since walking through the sanctuary doors, I get it. I at last comprehend the damning truth. No matter how long I'm a part of Living Waters, no matter how hard I pray or how many times I repent, there will be no conversion for me. The best I can hope for is resolve not to act on an intimate relationship with another woman, to *abstain*, and thereby avoid sinning. But there is no promise of authentic feelings of heterosexuality. My chest tightens. This whole thing and the better part of three years of my life have essentially been a lie. I can feel my airway constricting. Whether intentionally or not, this program has misled me into believing I can be made into the one thing I most certainly cannot—straight.

"You will need to sign and date the form and then Nina and I will sign as witnesses," I hear Dawn saying.

But I've already begun separating, peeling off my outer body, pulling free, floating away. As Dawn and Nina wait, I struggle to gather my splintering pieces. Then, without warning, I begin to feel something different. I feel angry. I merge once again with my physical body.

"And what happens if I don't sign?" I wonder if I sound as rabid as I feel.

Dawn's surprise is obvious as she drops her hand, the pen still clenched between her fingers. "Then we will have to ask you to leave Living Waters until you *are* willing to sign."

I look at Nina, focus on her eyes, on the way her lips press into a thin line, on her hands clasped together so tightly they appear white, the blood having drained out of the knuckles. I wait for her as a "former lesbian" to support me with at least a modicum of sympathy for the agony she must understand I'm feeling. She doesn't. I stand then, train my eyes solely on Nina.

"Then I will have to quit." I resist the urge to run.

I walk deliberately away, push open the sanctuary doors. I'm blasted with a gust of cool air. I wrap my arms tightly around me and hurry to the truck. Not until I've slid behind the wheel and slammed the door shut do I begin to shake. I cover my face with my hands and cry. *What now? What the fuck now?* Living Waters was my one last hope. Now I have no hope at all. I wipe my nose on my sleeve and start the truck. The parking lot has already emptied. Any minute, Dawn and Nina will likely make their way out of the church to their cars. I start the truck and heat surges through the cab. I roll straight through the vacant lot, driving over parking curbs as if I were in a monster truck. The drive home is less than thirty minutes by way of the freeway. But where I should turn right, I turn left, away from the freeway, steering instead toward Chuckanut Drive. Carved into a rocky hillside bordered by steep slopes and cliffs with views of the bay, this road is considered one of Bellingham's most scenic attractions. As teens, Chet and I raced his motorcycle along its bends and twists at perilous speeds. He taught me to lean into the curves with him and the bike as one unit. I loved riding with him, my arms wrapped tightly around his waist. The faster we drove, the more exhilarated and freer I felt. As I creep along the same route now, I feel anything but free. I feel alone, lost, empty, and I gravely consider driving off the side of the road. I imagine the truck flying over the edge of the pavement, smacking against and bouncing off of boulders before bursting into flames. With one move of the steering wheel, I can end my suffering for good. The truck's bumper thuds against something solid, I step on the brake. A guardrail. I've hit a guardrail, or rather, brushed it. Without realizing, I've slowed to a crawl. I shake my head, put the truck in reverse, turn around, and head for home.

seventeen

"Lorinda, can you tell me what happened?"

I wring my hands compulsively until they burn from the friction. The Beller sounds so far away, I wonder if we're still in the same room. I don't have the slightest idea how to answer her. I talked to Robin, got thrown out of Living Waters, that's all I really know. And now I don't know where to go, who to turn to. My skin is crawling, and I want out—out of my skin, my body, my life.

"Lorinda." Her face comes into focus.

Over the years, strands of gray have begun to feather her hair, but the soft skin of her face remains youthful. As always, she rocks in her chair, her shawl draped around her shoulders, notepad in her lap. Around me, stand the same dresser, bookshelf, and coffee table; I take refuge in their familiarity. I slide my shoes over the hardwood floor and am reminded of lying naked on another wood floor. The day Chet walked in on Robin and me, the day we were caught.

"She's here." I curl my hands into a ball in my lap.

"Who's here?"

I unfurl my hands, rub them up and down my thighs. "Robin," I whisper. My fingers are icicles, I shiver.

The Beller pulls an afghan from the back of her rocker, holds it out to me. I fold into the soft yarn and lean back against the couch. I cannot control the tears dripping now down my cheeks like rain from a gutter.

"Do you mean here in Bellingham?" She waits.

When my tears subside, she hands me a tissue, I blow my nose.

"You've missed her, haven't you?" She's tender as she leans into me, attempting to meet my eyes, but I can't look at her.

I feel like such an idiot, so naïve. I was so sure Living Waters would work, so sure if I prayed hard enough . . . I laugh, a short, quick laugh, and the Beller smiles.

"Have you talked to anyone in your church program?"

She barely finishes her question before I break into a fresh round of sobs. "I got kicked out!"

The Beller tilts her head to the side. "Tell me more."

But what more can I say? I've operated for three years under the assumption I could be converted. That I wasn't doomed to live as a sinful homosexual. That with enough work, enough prayer, I could be transformed into a faithful, heterosexual wife, and then my issues with adultery would fall away, too. But now this dream has been shattered because I'll never *feel* straight. The most I can hope for is resolve not to give in to my hidden desires. That's all anyone, even God, can offer me. I'm broken, eternally flawed, less than my fellow Christian sisters, and to avoid sin, I'll have to live in denial of my authentic feelings for the rest of my life. This is the only way to hold my family together, to honor my husband and my God.

"I'm a cheater, an adulterer."

I want the Beller to agree with me. I need to be right about something. All I have to hold on to is my sinfulness and my need for salvation.

"Have you considered that you are not the only one responsible for what's going on in your marriage? That maybe your husband plays a part as well?" She speaks soothingly but her words only irritate me.

"All Chet's ever been is a good husband and father."

"Well, I would disagree," she replies calmly. "In fact, I would even go so far as to suggest that at times he has been abusive." She turns toward her desk. "I have a name and number I would like to give to you." She pulls open a file cabinet.

I hold my arm across my chest as if to hold in my pounding heart. I know she's wrong. Chet isn't abusive. He's my husband, after all, and, if anything, my sin has caused him to be harsh at times.

When the Beller finds the sheet, she hands it to me. "Domestic Violence and Assault Services," she says. "No one has the right to force you to do anything you don't want to do. Not even your husband."

I nod, fold the paper in half, say goodbye. Then I walk straight to the bathroom where I crumple the paper with the help-line number and toss it into the trash can. The Beller means well, but she doesn't know how Christian marriage works. She doesn't understand that I don't have the luxury of living by whatever rules feel right for me. I belong to God and must live by his rules, whether that leads to personal happiness or not, for the Bible is full of self-sacrificing individuals giving up pleasure for obedience.

But in the days following my appointment with the Beller, I wrestle with the idea of Chet as abusive. He outwardly behaves as a fairy-tale husband and father. He coaches his boys' sports teams, visits them at their schools for lunch, and volunteers for field trips as a chaperone. The kids in the neighborhood excitedly gather in the cul-de-sac at every opportunity when he's out playing with Michael and Taylor, and there doesn't appear to be one mother at either of our boys' schools that doesn't adore him. He tells me he loves me all the time. Tells me he'd die without me; I am all he's ever wanted. As I mentally list his many attributes, I feel guiltier than ever for the impression of him I've left with the Beller. His sexual insistence is my failure of duty, how can I blame him? My body and his are one, they are supposed to have been one since we married. But what if I could tell him no? What if my body were mine to keep or give away to whom I wanted? My mind wanders to thoughts of Robin.

I normally teach a couple of fitness classes back-to-back, bolt across the street to grab a Starbucks latte, then dart back across to the gym. I then have approximately twenty minutes until my first client in which to down my sixteen ounces of liquid energy. This must last me until I can get home to grab a bite before picking the kids up from school. Within minutes of finishing a high-intensity workout class, my body cools down to shiver mode. I have three layers on top and two on the bottom and still I wrap my bare hands around my steaming coffee cup, attempting to soak up every bit of warmth. I feel my phone vibrate in my coat pocket, but don't want to pull my hands away to look. I sip at my coffee, feel the searing heat travel all the way down to my stomach. When my phone vibrates again, I know I should look. I pull it from my pocket, flip it open.

"Hey darlin'," reads the text message from Robin. "I'm in town visiting my family. Can I see you?"

I feel a cold sweat prickle my skin, I'm chilled all over again. She's *here*, here. I stare at the text, read it over. Here in *this* town and I can see her if I want to. I still have two people to train, but I *can* cancel. I can say I'm sick, or I have an emergency. Lost in thought, I jump when my phone vibrates again.

"Let me know," she texts, "I have to head back soon."

I can feel my anxiety level rising. What if this is the only chance I'll ever have again? Before my conscience can come up with all the reasons meeting her is wrong, I send Robin back a message.

"Meet me at Barnes & Noble in fifteen minutes."

Then I send my clients each a quick note, grab my coffee, and let the kid behind the front desk know I'll not be back for the day. I push open the gym doors and hold myself back from sprinting to my car. Barnes & Noble is directly across the street from the gym, and in a matter of minutes, I've pulled into the parking lot and found a spot close to the front door. I turn off the engine. I need to sit for a moment to calm my breathing. The lot isn't full of cars, but through the windows, the store appears to be hopping with people. Finally, I unhook my seatbelt. Inside, I walk directly to the Starbucks counter. The café is busy, the line loops around the tables. I scan the room but don't recognize anyone. The baristas are efficient, and soon I have another steaming latte in my hands. I find a seat away from the other tables and next to the window. The sun streams through and relaxes my tense muscles. I drink my coffee and close my eyes.

"Howdy, darlin'."

I open my eyes and Robin is standing in front of me, her lips turned up in a half-smile. I stand, she draws me into her arms. When she finally pulls back, I have a chance to really look at her. The first thing I notice is that her hair is almost completely gray. We sit across from each other, and Robin reaches over and squeezes my hand. I glance nervously over my shoulder.

"I don't think I've been followed." Robin grins.

She gestures toward the Starbucks' counter, gets up to put in an order. I watch her walk away from me; she's limping slightly on her left leg. I can't see her face but by the smile on the barista's, I can be certain Robin has said something charming. The barista giggles. Robin returns with a piping cup of coffee and settles back into her chair. She stares at me and I stare at her. We both look out the window and then at each other again. Robin speaks first.

"Well, how are ya?" She takes a sip of coffee.

I'm exhilarated, terrified, confused . . . I shrug.

"The weather was crappy on the way here," she continues.

I nod.

A couple walks over and stands near the window we are sitting at. I'm instantly anxious. I want them to move. The couple finally wanders off. In the absence of conversation on my part, Robin is filling me in on the details of her life. She's explaining that in the next couple of weeks, she'll be leaving Idaho and moving closer to home. She is moving to Tacoma, about two hundred miles south of where her family lives . . . and where I live, too.

"Why are you moving?" I pick at an imaginary piece of lint on my workout pants.

"Cuz I'm getting old," she laughs. "With this arthritis pain in my hip, I'm no good for farm work anymore."

Instead, she needs a more manageable, single-floor dwelling closer to town. Thanks to her previous barista experience, she's been hired by a Starbucks in Tacoma, and, as luck would have it, she has a friend who's asked her to move in as well. Robin pauses, drinks a mouthful of coffee, smiles. Why do I feel my stomach sink? Of course she has a friend.

"Ugh! I haven't given you a chance to speak!" She leans forward.

I shift my gaze down to the table. My emotions are doing cartwheels. I want to hug her, or yell at her, or cry or . . . I look up and her eyes meet mine. I'm unbearably weary of the numerous secrets I hold. I want to tell her. The couple meanders back this time with books in their hands. They lean up against the window chatting and flirting. The girl props her foot up on the wall behind her and the guy leans in until his head is touching her chin. Good grief, of all the places to huddle, right behind us is the place they choose.

"Honey, what is it?" Robin's voice draws me back.

But I don't know what to say. There is no light-hearted, easy place to start. At least not for me.

"I've tried so hard to live my life right for my kids, for Chet . . ." I say, my voice cracking.

"I know," she soothes, "I know."

"But I'm awful, totally awful."

She shakes her head.

I let a couple of tears fall, then wipe my face with my sleeve. The couple has left again, but I'm not taking any chances. I scoot my chair around and lean in as close to Robin as I can.

"Tell me. It's okay."

And whether it's a good idea or not, I cannot hold in the darkness I've hidden for so long. I tell her of my affairs with men, many men. I want her to understand that I never wanted any of them. Tears begin to fall from her eyes, too, as I try to explain Living Waters. How it was supposed to work, why I attended, and how I got kicked out.

"Oh baby." She pulls my head to hers and I let her.

I want to fall into her arms, let her shield me from the world. I hate the world. I hate being without her. She lifts my chin.

"When are you going to accept that you are like me and that we are okay?"

Her words are filled with compassion, her face full of warmth, and yet, I instinctively stiffen. Robin sits back slightly. Her eyes narrow in confusion. I stand too quickly, ungracefully, knock the table with my knee. I should have known she would say this. But she's wrong.

"I am not gay!"

I grab my wallet and half run, trying not to trip, down the magazine aisle. I'm sure people are staring. I head straight for the bathroom. I shove open an empty stall door and unravel a hand full of toilet paper. I dab at my eyes, blow my nose. *What the fuck am I doing?* Nothing has changed for me. I'm not any more available to run off with her today as I was ten years ago. The truth is,

I will never be available to run off with her. I flush the wad of toilet paper. I barely hear the wooden lavatory door creak open. Robin pushes her way inside my stall and slides the lock. I draw in a deep breath. She takes my face in her hands, cocks her head slightly then kisses me on the lips. I taste coffee on her tongue. Her body presses against mine. She slides her hand up the back of my shirt, under the band of my bra and unhooks the clasp; my breasts fall free.

"You sure about that, darlin'?" She backs me up against the wall.

Her hand creeps down the front of my workout pants. Her fingers explore my dampening folds. An involuntary moan escapes from my lips. What I know for sure is that I'm not sure about anything anymore.

eighteen

Chet and I have barely conversed all week. Since leaving Living Waters, my life has slipped all too easily back into a chaotic mess. As a result, I've given up trying to stay faithful to my marriage. I can no longer sustain the effort without the hopeful promise of a miraculous transformation to reach for. And now with Robin a mere phone call away, my longing for her combined with my Living Waters failure has created an intense resentment in me. I'm beginning to hate Chet. Today I breezed through a solo jog and headed straight for the coffee stand. Saturdays are the one day of the week I can go for a run and get coffee without having to rush home.

The aroma of freshly ground coffee beans wafts into the cab, I idle at the Starbucks drive-up window. The barista appears, hands me my coffee. My hands circle around the warm cup. I lift it to my lips and hear my cell phone ring. I hold my coffee gingerly in one hand while maneuvering open the glove box with the other. I cradle the phone between my ear and shoulder.

"Hello."

"So, I spoke with the bank yesterday." Chet's voice is flat.

"Good morning to you, too," I mumble. I pay the barista, then pull through and park in the adjoining lot.

"What about?" Again, I bring the steaming coffee to my lips.

"We've lost the house," Chet states flatly.

"What?" My airway fills with coffee.

I choke, fumble the cup. Hot coffee flies through the cab, splatters the windshield and hits the floor. I quickly reach down to mop up what I can with the two napkins the barista has given me.

"Just come home," he mumbles before he hangs up.

My phone slips from where I have it cradled between my ear and shoulder, lands in the coffee mess on the floor. *How can he lose a whole house?* I scoop up the drippy phone, deposit it onto the passenger seat, and head home.

Money has always been a contentious topic between Chet and me, mostly because I don't fully trust him to manage ours. For this reason, up until recently, I oversaw our finances. Making ends meet is a constant juggling act. Chet spends money faster than we make it, and no amount of explaining, pleading, or yelling on my part works to get his spending under control. Which is why one day, at my wits end, I threw the bills and checkbook register into Chet's lap.

"I quit! You take over!"

He didn't object, and, for the first time in fifteen years, our finances were in his hands. Once under his control, I rarely see a physical bill, as Chet always retrieves the mail before I do. He sets up many of our bills to be paid online, but doesn't share the passwords with me. If I question him, he blows me off, assuring me I have nothing to worry about. Once or twice, I come home from work to find a notice stuck to the door warning we're late on our mortgage. Panicked, I approach him, but he assures me he's working with a loan company on a modification loan. But this information does nothing to calm my fear. Again, he placates me with a story.

"This is just how things are. Mortgage loans are out of control and everyone is having to refinance," he says.

I know from what I've heard on the news that Chet's claim are, to some extent, true. In the years leading up to the sub-prime mortgage crisis, the US received large amounts of foreign money from fast-growing economies in Asia and oil-producing and exporting countries. This influx of funds, combined with low US interest rates from 2002 to 2004, contributed to loans of various types becoming easier to obtain. Consumers like Chet and me were approved for and assumed an exceptional debt load we couldn't realistically afford or manage. In 2002, we bought our house on an adjustable mortgage interest rate rather than a fixed one. Our parents warned us that securing anything other than a fixed loan was risky, but the bank assured us we could always refinance later. By the time the interest came due and we needed to refinance or come up with the money to pay considerably higher payments than we had been, the United States was in a full-on sub-prime mortgage crisis. We couldn't afford to refinance. We couldn't afford to pay higher payments. But instead of sharing this information with me and tackling our housing and financial problems together, Chet lied to me. He told me communication was slow between the finance company he was working with and the bank that owned our mortgage, but reassured me we had no reason to worry. This should have been my clue to worry, I know better than that.

Driving home from Starbucks after Chet's call, my hands shake on the steering wheel, as much with anger as with fear. *This is your fault, you liar! You never think about anyone but yourself!* I hurl accusations at him in my mind while ignoring a tinge of nagging guilt. *Aren't I as much a liar as he is?* Normally, I placate myself with the idea that I'm at least working on my issues through counseling, prayer, and confession. *What's he doing besides spending all our money and losing our house?* I turn the corner into our neighborhood, feel the truck labor under the incline. I push the gas pedal to the floor. The truck is a ridiculous beast that Chet *had* to have. He promised he would drive it to work every day, but he rarely does, because instead he fell in love with a shiny Mercedes that he cannot be without. I can feel my anger building, mounting as I climb the hill. By the time the roof of our house comes into view, my anger has engulfed me. I explode through the front door in pursuit of Chet and find him standing lifeless in front of the fireplace, his face pale.

"What the fuck happened?" I charge him like a bull, stopping just short of bumping into him.

"Lorinda, I'm sorry." He holds his hands in front of him, prayer like. "We fell behind on our mortgage payments."

"Well, no shit!" I shriek.

"Lorinda, I swear, the loan company turned out to be fraudulent. They took our money. It's not my fault!" And there it is, the lie. I know it when I hear it, but I so desperately want to believe him that I snatch up his excuse.

Exasperated, Chet throws his hands in the air, walks out of the room. I don't have the energy to go after him and instead fall heavily into the loveseat. I lean my head into the couch cushions, my gaze lands on the fireplace mantel, my showcase for holiday decorations, photos, and candles. My eyes fill with tears as I study the brightly painted wall behind, the carefully hung family photos, and the shelves Chet made for my birthday. I tilt my head a little further back, smile at the faint pin holes just barely visible in the ceiling. Years earlier, I had jammed my bra into the drain of the sink, faucet still running. This caused water to rush over the counter, soaking the floor and drip through to the living room ceiling. After drilling pin holes into the ceiling to relieve the water pressure, Chet held up my dripping bra.

"Boys, this is why we don't wash our bras in the sink," he playfully announced.

I laugh out loud as I remember the scene, then bury my face in my hands and sob. Oh God, the boys! How will we tell the boys? This isn't merely a house; this is the only home my kids have known, and now what? Where will we go?

Even in the most challenging of times, as the world crumbles, even then, the job of a faithful Christian mother and wife is to protect her children and support her husband. I know this, but I want someone to protect me. I need someone to tell me everything will be all right even though I feel sure nothing ever will be again. I want to blame Chet, I want to blame God, but I know the blame is mine, my unfaithfulness has brought us to this place. I know I must fight to maintain a sense of normalcy for Michael and Taylor's sake, but our impeding eviction hangs overhead, an ominous cloud of despair and unknowing until even physical exercise, my trustworthy release from the stress of life, is not enough to cure my grief.

I leave a message for the Beller, then I text Aaron. He meets me in our usual spot, and I fill him in on what's happened. I explain as much as I can, as much as I know, but he's skeptical.

"Are you sure Chet is being honest with you?"

I'm stunned by his doubt. "Of course! He doesn't want to lose our house, either!"

Aaron nods, but I can tell he's placating me.

"If I can do anything to help . . ." He folds me in a hug, and it feels good to be wrapped in his arms.

I pretend for a minute he can protect me from impending doom. We don't sneak off the trail into the woods, he just holds on to me until I'm ready to let go. And when we part, he makes me promise to keep him posted.

My visits with the Beller are sporadic, but I keep a journal that I hand over to her when we do meet. She rocks in her chair, quietly reads through my words, then asks me questions. This has been our rhythm now for years. I don't say much out loud, but I've written hundreds of pages and she's kept them all.

I watch as her eyes widen, and I imagine she must be reading about the house. I pick at an invisible string on my jacket.

"Wow, Lorinda. I am so sorry. How are you doing?" she lays my writing down in her lap.

I shrug.

"Have you and Chet spoken with a bank or is there anyone who can help?"

I feel my eyes cloud with tears. "I did this," I whisper.

"What did you do?" She stops rocking, pulls herself closer to the couch.

I stare at the ground, let the tears slide off my nose. "All of it," I choke out. This is all my fault and now God is punishing my family.

"Lorinda, this is not your fault." She gets up from her rocker, kneels in front of me. "Can you look at me?"

I don't want to look at her. I'm too ashamed. I don't deserve her kindness.

"This is not your fault. You did not cause this." The beads of her necklace clink together as she reaches out to lift my chin.

But I know the truth. Still, I wish I were a better person, I wish I were the person the Beller thinks I am.

The only thing to do is to go about pretending life is normal, even though no one is fooled, especially not Michael and Taylor. My number one fear is for them. I grew up in the same house my entire childhood. I went to school in the same school district and had the same friends my whole life. I had stability in that way, and I want that same stability for my kids. For them, I hold my breath, hoping somehow, some way we will save our house. I try not to spew my tragic news to everyone I see, but when a woman in my cycling class inquires as to how I'm doing, I dissolve into tears. Fairly new to my classes, Sandy is maybe ten or fifteen years older than me, and fit. She has graying hair that bounces wildly around her face when she rides. She's always overflowing with energy and a positive attitude. I choke on my tears and manage to recount my sad tale to her in bits and pieces.

"Oh no!" Sandy wipes the sweat from her forehead, rests her hand on my shoulder. "Maybe I can help."

"Oh, no . . ." I wipe my face, but Sandy holds up her hand.

"Look, I'm a lawyer. Maybe I can help." She offers to come to our house and look over our loan paperwork.

Though real estate is not her area of law, she's willing to offer whatever insight she can. I feel a flicker of hope and I jump at her offer. But when I call Chet, asking him to gather all of the documents related to the loan, he sounds less than enthusiastic.

"There probably isn't anything she can do." His annoyance makes me anxious.

"Maybe, but it's worth a try." I hang up before he can protest further.

A couple of hours later, Sandy sits, crossing and uncrossing her feet as she reads and rereads the stack of papers we've dumped into her lap.

"I'll need to do some research to find out more about this modification loan," she says. "In the meantime, let me see if we can meet with the new owner. If we can work out a rental situation, you may not have to move right away." As she looks around our house, I watch her smile slowly fade. "It just makes me sick that this can happen. I am so sorry for you."

I feel the tears well up inside of me and I glance at Chet. He's staring at the floor, stoic. Sandy stands, as do I.

"I'll talk to you soon," she assures me. Then, she holds her hand out to Chet where he remains seated. "Nice meeting you."

He takes her hand but says nothing.

Sandy leaves, and I no sooner shut the door behind her when Chet blurts, "Is she a lesbian?"

I'm taken aback. Where did that come from? "I don't know."
I shrug.

"I think she is."

He leaves the room without another word.

A few days later, Sandy calls to say she's arranged a meeting
with the owner. I cringe at the thought that someone else owns
my house. She advises us to "make nice" with him. She hopes to
find out if he intends on living in the house or renting it. If his
intentions are to rent, we could attempt to persuade him to rent
to us. I feel sick to my stomach. How is it we must convince a
stranger to let us live in our own house? We agree to meet at the
Starbucks down from our house.

I sit with my back to the coffee shop's crackling fireplace. I'm
unable to shake the chill that's crept into my bones. Sandy and
Chet sit on either side of me. Chet stares at the ground, a scowl
on his lips. Sandy holds a cup of coffee, sips quietly while we wait.
A bell chimes and a long-limbed, hardened looking man ambles
through the door carrying a worn messenger bag over one shoulder. He wears grimy overalls and hefty work boots. He stares
directly at Chet, bobs his head in greeting. Chet comes out of his
chair, shakes the man's hand. I feel Sandy's eyes on me.

Sandy reaches out her hand. "I'm Sandy. Thank you for agree-
ing to meet with us."

"Paul," the man replies, taking hold of her hand.

"As I told you on the phone, I'm a good friend of this couple's."

Paul sits silently, unmoving.

Sandy continues. "The reason for meeting is to inquire about your intentions for the house. If your plan is to rent it, they'd like to be considered as possible renters."

Paul folds both his hands on the table, exhales slowly. I hold my breath; Chet looks down at the table. Paul clears his throat and I glance up at him. I can feel tears, but I hold them back.

"Yes, well . . ." His voice is taut. "My daughter is moving in."

I start to cry. That's it then, we have no chance of staying in our home.

Not yet ready to give up, Sandy leans in closer to Paul. "What you are likely unaware of is the fact that this couple was forced out of their home," she implores. "They were deceived by a fraudulent loan company and lost their house where they've lived with their children for over ten years."

Paul squares his shoulders, sits taller. "I'm a good Christian man," he replies. "I'm not in the business of throwing families into the street." He looks at Chet. "I bought this house from an auction. I'm sorry you've lost it, but . . ."

I begin to bawl louder. Customers turn, gawk in our direction. Sandy presses her car keys into my hand. I snatch the keys, turn on Chet.

"*You* will tell our children! *You* will!" I shove open the door. It catches in the wind, bangs into the side of the building.

My cheeks are on fire, the cold air merely dissipates against my skin. I find Sandy's car, get inside. I toss the keys onto the dash. I slam my back against the seat. I do it again. Over and over, I fling myself against the seat as I scream. By the time Chet and Sandy return to the car, I've cooled down and am once again freezing.

Sandy opens the driver's side door and gets in. Chet climbs into the backseat without a word.

Sandy takes a deep breath. "Well, this didn't go as we'd hoped, but you will get through it," she says. "Losing a house is not worth losing your marriage for."

Her words fall like bricks. Chet gets out of the car. I thank Sandy and follow him.

After the unsuccessful meeting with Paul, time speeds up. Paul wants us out of the house as soon as possible. Another tidal wave of anguish hits, and I rely on friends and family who show up, offering help. My emotions are erratic, unpredictable. One second I'm carefully tucking dishes between towels, stacking them neatly into boxes, and the next, I'm hurling wine glasses at the kitchen wall. My cousin, Jerrie, takes my behavior in stride, allowing me space to grieve. But after the third glass I toss goes sailing past Jerrie's head, she calmly picks up the shards of glass and points me away from the kitchen.

Nine-year-old Taylor trails me, recording the house with his cell phone camera. He follows me into the master bedroom, where he films the vinyl quote I'd pressed into the wall above our family pictures. "We may not have it all together, but together we have it all," it reads. My heart breaks as I watch this once concrete piece of Taylor's world crumble and fall away. I place my hands gently on his shoulders, turn him around, back out of my bedroom. He moves on, filming the hallway, the laundry room, his bedroom. In the master bedroom, I look around one last time. The once bright and cheerful curtains I selected now hang heavily against the windows. The walls appear stark, pocked with nail holes and flaking sheetrock dust. The vanity lights glare back angrily from above the bathroom mirror. I look away. I leave my bedroom, stop one last time in each of the boys' bedrooms. I remember their excited faces the day we moved in. How they ran in circles, laughing and whooping. I walk down the stairs and can't help but think of Christmas morning. The boys flinging themselves down the steps into an ecstatic heap under the Christmas tree, impatiently waiting for Chet and me to catch up. I step off the bottom step, peer across the dining room into the kitchen. My vast assortment of coffee mugs, refrigerator magnets, antique mason jars, and numerous other collectables decorated the room just hours ago . . . just hours ago . . . now, the house is empty. Empty of furniture, people, and life. I climb into my mammoth, longbox truck and glance in the rearview mirror. Michael and Taylor sit hunched forward with their heads in their hands, too weary, too grief-stricken to even look up. I start the truck, let it idle for a moment, then pull forward. I watch as the garage doors close behind me and whisper a silent farewell as I drive away for the last time.

nineteen

We find a rental house on the outskirts of town not far from a lake. With gleaming hardwood floors and granite countertops, a fireplace in the master bedroom, and jetted bathtubs in the bathrooms, under different circumstances, it would easily be our dream home. The house is brand new, never rented or lived in. I'm thankful we'll be the first family here. I want this place to feel like home to my shell-shocked children as quickly as possible. I put their room together, first making it as familiar as I can, but in my heart, I feel I'm merely playing house. An irrational place in my mind holds fast to the hope that I'll wake up in my own house, in my own neighborhood, where I belong. My whole being aches for where I've come from rather than where I've ended up. And how did I end up here, exactly? Chet snaps when I ask him for money to buy groceries or gas.

"I told you we don't have money," he huffs impatiently.

But when I pry for more information as to where the money is going, he simply stomps off without answering. Even after spending considerable time looking over the paperwork Chet has provided her; Sandy has no idea as to what happened with our house. I want her to find something in the loan papers that will get our house back or, at the very least, get some of our money back. At Sandy's request, I ask Chet if maybe there are documents he's forgotten to include with those he gave her.

"Jesus, Lorinda," he exhales sharply, "just forget it. Let it go. The house is gone."

But I can't let it go. How can I? That house is our home and if there is any way at all Sandy can get us back home, I want to know.

The next day, after Chet has gone to work and I've dropped both kids off at school, I drive to Sandy's office where she has agreed to meet with me on her lunch break. She occupies a small space on the first floor of the Bellingham Towers, tucked between a conference room and another office. Her office is less formal than I imagined. Behind her desk is a wall of books sprinkled with awards and thank-you cards. One in particular catches my eye: LGBT Advocate Award. Sandy smiles, takes her glasses off. I sit down across from her.

"Are you actually aware of the status of your finances?" Sandy asks.

What does she mean by that? I feel my cheeks flush with embarrassment.

"That's where I'd begin if I were you," she states in a tone that is matter-of-fact.

I'm not sure how to respond. When I try to find my voice, I realize it's gone, slipped away like it so often has before in the presence of the Beller, when I feel unsure and small. My hands sweat as I clasp them tighter together in my lap.

"I'm not accusing anyone of anything," Sandy says, "but *if* Chet has been at all untruthful about where your money has gone, you have a right to know."

I feel my stomach twist at the word "untruthful." I'm untruthful, unfaithful. But Chet has withheld vitally important information about what's going on with our mortgage, leaving me blindly trusting as we hurl headfirst toward homelessness. Anyway, I no longer know the passwords on our accounts, and asking Chet will surely send up a red flag.

As if reading my mind, Sandy leans forward. "Stop by the bank on your way home and ask to change your passwords," she says. "It's as simple as that."

I take in a deep breath and thank her, but I know nothing with Chet is ever simple. I walk back to the truck, weighing Sandy's suggestion over in my mind. A sinking feeling in my gut warns me I may be walking into a world of hurt if I pursue this. But I can't help picturing Michael and Taylor. They've already been through so much, and if there is even the slightest chance we can get our house back, I owe them that. I start the engine, check my rear-view mirror. A woman waits to cross the parking lot, a toddler wrapped tightly in her arms. We make eye contact; she smiles over the child's head. She remains, as a good mother does, to be certain I'm stopped completely, that she can cross safely. I smile back, nod my head. She hurries quickly across, and I know what I have to do.

It takes less than five minutes to get the passwords on our bank accounts reset. Still, panic courses through my veins the entire drive home. I sit down on the couch with my laptop, log in to our checking account. My throat tightens as I scroll slowly through hundreds of dollars of withdrawals for restaurants, bars, flower shops, and spas—none of which have been enjoyed by me. And I know, of course I know, Chet has found someone else.

When he returns home from work that night, he's primed for me to confront him. He sits down at the kitchen table stone-faced. My voice wavers as I ask him if he has an explanation for the banking activity I've brought up on the screen. He does not have an explanation and he's furious I'm questioning him. Then, I ask if he is seeing someone and he detonates.

"I've never had an affair! You have no right to accuse me!" He stomps down the stairs, shoves open the door to our bedroom.

I trail him closely, I can't let him drop this, I must know what's going on. Chet weaves around the boxes we've yet to unpack and disappears into the oversized closet.

"Where's our money?"

He emerges from the closet with a suitcase. My mouth hangs in disbelief as he rips clothes from hangers and tosses them in the suitcase.

"No," I beg, reaching out to him; he shoos me away like I'm a bug. "Chet," I plead, "in seven more years, Taylor will be out of school . . . can't you—"

"I've wasted the best years of my life on you!" he cuts me off. "No, I will not wait seven more years!" His glare is fierce.

"Please don't leave, Chet," I slide down to my knees in front of him.

"Why not?" he bites back. "You did. Years ago."

I cringe. He's not wrong, I did leave. Or maybe I never actually showed up. Chet steps around me, grabs his keys from the dresser. Wound in a ball on the floor, I hear his Mercedes tear out of the garage.

It's after midnight when he returns. He climbs into bed without a word and soon I hear the steady rhythm of his breathing. I lay awake, unable to calm the shaking that's crept into my limbs. I get up, quietly layer on warm, fuzzy pajamas and socks, but still I shiver. I turn on the gas fireplace, watch as the flames flicker to life around the faux logs. I curl up on the floor, wait for the heat to permeate my trembling body. At some point I drift off, and when I awake, Chet is gone again.

He returns home after work each night, or I presume he's working; I'm no longer sure of anything. He's already changed the passwords to our bank accounts again, but it doesn't matter, we're broke anyway. The next few weeks pass in a blur. We don't speak. Then one night, I come home from work and find every photo of me face down on our bedroom dresser. Only the pictures with me in them are facedown. When I question him, Chet flies into a rage.

"I can't move on as long as *you're* here," he spits, venom dripping from his voice. He paces back and forth, darting glances in my direction, rubbing his hands down his pant legs.

I suck in my breath. "What are you saying?" I back up against a wall, will my voice to remain calm.

He turns toward me, plants his hands on either side of my head, brings his face within inches of mine. "If you weren't so beautiful, it'd be so much easier to leave you." He covers my lips with his.

When he pulls away, his eyes are wild. I search desperately for a glimpse of the man I know; I must find him. I can't lose him. Not now, not after all we've lost. I can fix this, whatever this is. I'm meant to be his wife and I will keep him. Without a word, I slide slowly down the wall. His eyes follow, penetrating mine as I unbutton his pants, reach inside his underwear, take him in my mouth.

Chet remains distant, but he's quit making mention of leaving. We sleep in the same bed most nights, but the blow job is our last bit of physical contact. He works all the time, including weekends and overnight, which I know is implausible, yet I can't allow myself to imagine where he is or with whom. Money is in short supply. Chet hasn't admitted to his affair, but how else can I explain the money spent on flowers, hotels, and Gucci bags, none of which have come my way? So, when he informs me he'll be leaving for union officer training in Louisiana for a week, I hold out my open palm to him.

"What do you want?"

"I want the money for rent."

"The management company said we can pay when I return." He pushes past me.

"Really, Chet?" I don't hide my skepticism.

"Yes, Lorinda." He throws his stuff into the back of his car. He yells goodbye to the boys, speeds off.

I go back into the house, back to the laundry I'm folding.

I don't question why the aluminum smelter is sending a brick-layer to a union meeting in Louisiana. Is Chet even a union officer? I honestly don't know. But it doesn't really matter. I'm living in a time warp and I must hang on, wait for everything to smooth back out. Things *will* go back to normal; they have to. I wait for Chet to call and let me know he's made it safely to Louisiana, but he doesn't. I try to call him, but his phone sends me directly to voice mail.

A few days after he's gone, I return home from picking up the boys from school and spot the yellow slip, glowing like a caution light, from the front door. I jump out of the car, rip the note from the door. As the reality of what I'm reading sinks in, my body turns cold, fear engulfing me once again. This is an eviction notice. We are being evicted and Chet is gone. Not knowing who else to turn to, I dial Chet's parents. My own parents are out of town, visiting relatives in Illinois. Jo answers on the first ring.

"Mom . . ." I break into sobs.

"What is it, hon'? Hang on, Dad and I are coming."

I sniff back my tears, get back into the car with the boys. I arrange to have my in-laws pick them up and take them home with them. I don't know what I'm going to do, but I can't bear to tell the kids we've been evicted. I tell them to go in and pack clothes because Grandma and Grandpa are coming to get them. They look at each other and then me. They've never slept over at their grandparents' house. To be fair, I don't let them stay many places. I'm overly protective; I know no one can take better care of them than I can—could—now, I'm not so sure.

"Go!" I yelp excitedly, and the boys dash for the house.

By the time they're packed into Butch and Jo's truck, I'm in full panic mode. I thank them for taking the boys, assure them I'll be in touch. They know better than to ask what's wrong, instead Butch envelopes me in a hug.

"Love ya, sugar." He kisses me on the cheek. "You take your time; we've got the boys."

I thank him again, watch as they back out of the driveway. I stand in front of my new house, evicted, and the energy drains from body. I have no idea what to do next. I smooth the notice out in my hand. I will call the number, try to explain, but first, I call Sandy.

"There was a notice on the door." I crumple the yellow slip between my fingers, I'm not sure what I expect her to do. I really don't know her well enough to expect she'll do anything. But I wait, hope.

"Okay," Sandy says. "Sit tight. I'm on my way."

She picks me up in her black Subaru and we drive to the management company that oversees our house rental. Chester, the manager, greets us warmly until Sandy tells him who I am. His demeanor chills as he informs us that he's never spoken with Chet directly.

"I do have copies of post-dated checks Chet dropped in the after-hours box," he said. "Of course, we do not accept post-dated checks, and though I've left several messages to that effect on Mr. Gebhart's voice mail, he's not responded."

My face burns with shame. I want to explain I had no idea we hadn't paid rent. I'm not the kind of person who doesn't pay her bills. But I don't have to because Sandy steps in.

"This is all new to Mrs. Gebhart. She's a victim here."

"They haven't made a payment in the four months they've lived there." Chester rubs his face, glances at mine. "Look, best I can do is give you two days to get your stuff out and get on your way."

I'm too stunned to comment, to even wrap my mind around what he's saying. Sandy shakes his hand, thanks him, guides me back outside. She holds firmly to my arm as we walk back to her car.

"We can get this done." She opens the door, helps me inside. "We just need to call some people to help."

In a whirlwind of action, I watch as friends and family come together to pack our twenty years of belongings into their trucks and cars. A recent training client, Mike, volunteers a unit at his storage company free of charge for as long as I need. He brings friends to help, U-Hauls to load, and takes charge of the situation. Under his expert supervision, the house is nearly empty by the end of the day. The afternoon of the second day, my father-in-law secures the final boxes in the bed of his truck, climbs into his cab. He holds his fingers in a farewell salute, backs out of the driveway. Sixteen-year-old Michael waves his grandfather on, then faces me.

"So, that's it then, we're homeless." The anger in his glare sends a shiver down my spine. "And we don't know where Dad is?"

I feel the weight of my son's devastation press in on me. At least Taylor is staying with his grandparents and will at least be spared the trauma of packing up yet again.

"No, we don't know where Dad is," I admit, "but we're not homeless. We're staying with Sandy." She has an extra room and lives close to the boys' schools and my job.

"But it's not *our* home." He kicks at the rocks for emphasis.

I swallow back tears. He's right, our home is gone, again, the second time in four months. We walk to Sandy's car; I shift my box to one arm as I rub at my eyes. We're fortunate Sandy has extended an invitation to stay with her, but it can't erase the feelings of being displaced. Except for the absolute essentials for daily living, everything we have has been hauled to Mike's storage business. Everyone and everything are gone, except for my son, me, and Sandy, who sits waiting in her idling car. I stop a few feet from the Subaru. Michael's expression softens as does his tone.

"Mom, it will be okay." He wraps an arm around my shoulder. It's strong, muscular like his father's. He's no longer a boy. His voice is deepening. And sadly, so is his understanding of the cruelties of life.

We drive to Sandy's house. I give up wiping the tears from my eyes, watch as the world passes by through my blurred vision, wondering if anything will ever be clear again.

After a full week of countless voice mails pleading him to call or text me, Chet ambles back into town. Both boys are upstairs tucked into the room they now share in Sandy's house. They've both withdrawn considerably from the world, hidden safely behind the walls they've built around their island of two. Their pain, so plainly etched into their young faces, tears through my heart every time I dare glance at them. I'd give anything to ease their misery. My mind plays, replays events that have taken place since Chet disappeared. I'm going mad. I wander to the porch swing in front of the house, sit. The swing sways back and forth in the breeze, I attempt to clear my head of chaos. When my cell phone rings, I retrieve it from my pocket. Chet's name flashes across the screen and I jam the phone against my ear.

"Where are you?" I yell, unable to keep the hysteria out of my voice.

"On the freeway. Coming home." Chet's patronizing tone sends me reeling.

"Home where?" I seethe. "We've been evicted!"

"Why didn't you just pay it?" he bites back.

What? Is he serious?

"Because you have all the money!" I scream so loudly my voice cracks.

"You could have borrowed it!" I toss the phone in the air as if it were on fire.

I leap from the porch swing so abruptly it hits me in the back of the legs. I drop to my knees, still hear Chet yelling my name from the phone as it flies across the deck. But I leave it where it lays, rest my face on the solid wood planks beneath me.

"Fuck you, Chet. Fuck you," I yell into the night.

twenty

Via Facebook, I find out that Chet never attended a union meeting in Louisiana. He was vacationing poolside in Las Vegas with his girlfriend.

"Dude, I got an email from your husband," my best friend, Aimee, almost whispers into the phone.

I feel my panic level rising. My body is now in a constant state of fight or flight. My stomach is forever in knots, my acid reflux is worse than when I was pregnant, and, to add insult to injury, my face is breaking out like a pubescent teenager's, which never actually happened when I was a teenager. Aimee clears her throat; I shift the phone into the crook of my neck. I log into my email account; Chet's email sits at the top of the list. I lean closer to the screen. *This can't be.* He's sent a letter to every email contact in our list: family, friends, clients, professional contacts, and, of course, to me.

His email begins with a list of his personal attributes, not un-like the achievements and awards section of a resume. He goes on to graphically expose my affair with Robin fifteen years earlier. He emphasizes the pain he's endured as a faithful, godly husband married twenty years to a closeted lesbian. He speaks of how he's prayed for my redemption, but alas, he's been pushed to his limit. He closes by asking for prayer for himself and his children. I gasp out loud. He isn't the strongest writer, proofreading his emails has always been my job. Still, his message is clear enough, and as the content begins to sink in, so does my fear.

"I got it, too," I finally reply.

"Have you seen Facebook?" she asks.

Reluctantly, I log in and find Chet's letter in its entirety.

Oh my God.

"It's going to be okay," Aimee promises. Best friends lie for each other's sake. "I know it seems like the end of the world, but it's not. Your parents don't have email or Facebook."

Panic grips my heart all over again as I picture the look on my parents' faces, my God-fearing, Bible-obeying, homophobic mother's face. What if she takes Chet's side? Maybe even helps him take my children from me. My mind races through my options for damage control. I can send my own letter denying everything. I'm a faithful woman of God, wife of twenty years. I have credibility! I hang up with Aimee, prepared to write my own letter. I begin by apologizing for Chet's behavior. Not only are our personal issues nobody's business, but neither does anyone need more drama in their lives. I explain that Chet and I are going through a rough patch and that we all say things in anger and that what he's claiming about me is obviously untrue. But then, I stop.

I pull my fingers away from the keyboard, reread what I've written.

What am I doing? Chet is gone. Our house is gone. Our money is gone. Our marriage is gone. I shut my laptop. Maybe this will blow over and I won't have to respond at all. Maybe Chet's email will end up in junk mail and people won't bother to read it. This is what I hope, what I pray. But within hours of Chet's letter, I begin receiving messages from people I consider friends, people I sit next to in church, stand alongside at school events, now sending accusatory, damning messages.

"Are you a lesbian now?"

"Seriously, you've been lying all this time?"

"You're a cheater!"

"You know being gay is against nature, right? You're going to Hell."

At first, I respond to each question, each accusation. I try to explain this isn't how it happened. My affair with a woman long ago can't be reason enough for Chet leaving us homeless and penniless now. But the messages flood in, ripping at my self-confidence, magnifying my own deep-seeded self-loathing until finally, I turn on myself. What kind of a mother am I really? One who jeopardizes her family by having affairs, and not just with Robin, but with men, too. What kind of a wife does that?

What am I thinking, anyway? I know there is no use in trying to beat Chet. Years of experience have taught me he'll come out looking the victim and I'll be exposed as the homosexual adulteress I am. Chet is a fan favorite, after all. Women in church, mothers from the kids' schools all love him. He always knows the right words to say, portrays himself as the doting husband and father; I feel more like his shadow than his partner. I know better than to defy him, because the unspoken condition is that whatever I do, must make Chet look good.

The aftershock of Chet's email reverberates through every aspect of my life. Whether actual or not, I'm positive every eye is on me—judging me in the drop-off circle at school, scrutinizing me as I stand in line at the grocery store or bank. And between accusatory text messages and the many people who've dropped me from Facebook, I feel alone, desperately alone. I'm a dismal disappointment, deserving of the situation I find myself in. I may have earned what's happening to me, but my children haven't. They deserve stability, happiness—things I can no longer provide.

Chet threatens to take the kids away from me. He tells me they want to be with him, because I'm a liar who has broken up our family. I believe him. I cannot bear the thought; the familiar desolation of depression hollows me until I ache with emptiness.

I'm surely coming down with a cold, my forehead is glistening with sweat from the effort of packing the boys' lunches. I haven't begun coughing yet, but my throat is raw, my head pounding. After dropping the kids at school, I'll drive straight to the gym and work out. I need to work out, I'll feel better. But as if being controlled by another set of hands, my car turns away from my usual route and is soon climbing a steep slope of a hill. I pull into a parking spot in Whatcom Falls Park, mindlessly place my car keys under the seat. I open the door, step out onto the wet pavement. It's cool outside, blustery, and long before the bridge comes into view, I can hear the roar of the waterfall. I walk across the bridge, follow the trail leading to the top of the falls, make my way to the bank's edge. The spray from the falls wets my face as the water thrashes against, then bounces off the rocks below. My foot slips as a dirt clod breaks free, sending beads of sweat down my neck, snaking between my shoulder blades. I swallow the golf ball in my throat, steady myself before moving closer to the edge. This can be the end of everything. No more guilt for my failing marriage. No more trying to get life right, only to be hit head-on by my own inadequacy. The ground shifts under my feet, loose rocks slip over the side of the bank. I readjust my weight, lean into the cooling mist, let it coat my skin with tiny droplets of moisture. My phone vibrates. I look to see that Sandy is calling. I answer her call, hear her yelling my name, but I don't have the energy to respond. Instead, I hold the phone in my hand, imagine those who will be affected by my death. My children, my biggest regret: to burden them with the death of their mother, the suicide of their mother, is cruel. But I can't help but believe they'll be better off without me. If I were straight, none of this would be happening. I close my eyes, imagine the rocks giving way to the crumbling bank. The roar of the falls is deafening as I imagine slipping on the wet moss, hitting my head on the sharp boulders below. The water will cover my face, fill my mouth and nose until I'm swallowing water faster than I can spit it out. Surely, the severe cold will render me unconscious, and I'll be pulled under by the force of the falls. Again, I hear my name being called. I open my eyes, look to my phone, bring it to my ear.

"Lorinda, where are you? Please, tell me where you are."

"The waterfall," I reply.

"Whatcom Falls?"

I pull the phone away from my ear, nod.

I turn away from the water then, take a couple steps away from the edge; my legs are shaking. *What the fuck am I doing?* I cover my face with my hands. I'm too scared to face the falls again, too depleted to make it back to my car. I hear my name, part my fingers, and think I see Sandy running in my direction. I wave at her, she waves back, orders me not to move. When she's in front of me, I all but collapse into her strong arms. She drags me away from the cliff.

"This isn't how it ends," she's shouting into my ear.

She has her arm around my waist. I can hear the rhythmic pounding of water behind me. Sandy half drags me to a car I've never seen before, the driver's door is still flung open in her haste to get to me.

"I had to borrow another lawyer's car because I rode my bike to work," Sandy explains.

She opens the passenger door; I drop into the leather seat. The car reeks of men's cologne, I can taste it on my tongue.

"Why would you do this, Lorinda? Why would you even consider this?"

I have nothing for her. I'm numb.

She continues talking, faster and louder. "I called your work to check on you, I just had this *feeling*. No one had seen you."

I stare mutely out the windshield.

Sandy drives us to her house. She helps me out of the car, up the stairs, into bed. I don't object, I don't say a word. The bedsheet is cool under my feverish cheek. I close my eyes. Immediately, Chet's face appears, his mouth set in a triumphant smirk. His misdeeds will be forgotten or at the least will take a backseat, but I will forever be known as sinful, fallen, and worst of all . . . as a lesbian. I'm ashamed of my weakness. I picture Michael and Taylor. I worry about what will happen to them now that everyone knows their mother has ripped their family apart. I wrap my arms tightly around my middle, as if to hold myself together.

twenty-one

Three months after being evicted, Sandy speaks with the owner of a small rental house next door to hers. She assures the owner I will be an excellent, dependable renter, and the owner is beyond thrilled not to have to deal with applications and vetting hassles.

The house is about eight hundred square feet in size, the same size of my first marital house, which coincidentally sits only a couple of blocks away from this one. The layout is nearly identical. I walk into the bedroom resembling the one I shared with Chet nearly twenty years earlier. In a flash, I see the unmade bed, Robin's and my clothes tossed carelessly on the floor. I hear the reverberation of the front door slamming. I cannot sleep in this room. I give it to Taylor and take the one at the end of the hall. Michael gets the basement bedroom.

Mom scrubs the kitchen and bathroom clean like only my mother can, and Sandy moves furniture while I set up the boys' bedrooms. Each item I unpack reminds me of the past. Not long ago I lived in *my* house, a house I believed I owned. These pieces of furniture, these photos, all belong in *that* house, not this one. I don't enjoy moving even under the best of circumstances. I prefer to nest, carving out a comfortable home for my family and staying put. This is our fourth move in less than five months.

"This is going to be so cute!" Mom remarks, as she spreads a tablecloth over the table.

I know she's trying to keep my spirits up, but my heart aches as I survey my life scattered about the house in half-empty boxes hastily thrown together during eviction. Though I took care to pack Chet's clothes, softball gear, and other personal belongings into separate boxes and send them home with his parents, I still pull out a sock here, a T-shirt there, and each time, I feel compelled to yell for him, let him know I found his stuff, but then I remember that he's moved in with his parents. He has nowhere else to go. He refuses to speak with me unless he's telling me what he wants or yelling at me for "taking everything." I can only assume he means the furniture, as every bank account we shared is now zeroed-out. He's spent every cent. Even the modest amount of money we were saving for our kids' future college expenses is gone.

When I'm contacted by the IRS and told that I owe years and years of back taxes, I finally turn to Sandy for help, and she advises me to file for a legal separation. She says that once this is done, our finances will become separate, and I'll be able to have my own account that he can't touch. As for the taxes, that's another story. Eventually, I'll have to hire a tax attorney to help me make a deal with the IRS.

Sandy mercifully convinces her friend to charge a third of what she can ask for in rent. As a fitness instructor and personal trainer, I make barely enough money to cover both the rent and my other expenses. Chet is unwilling to pay child support, even though we go to court several times. Each time the commissioner orders him to do so, Chet refuses. Chet is fired from Alcoa, which means the boys and I no longer receive medical or dental insurance. Fortunately, the kids can get on a state plan. I work as many hours as possible, but I can barely afford to keep food in the house. Reluctantly, I swallow my pride and apply for food stamps. I'm low, about as low as I can get, until Michael's German teacher approaches me. For over a year, Chet has led me to believe he's been making payments toward Michael's class trip to Germany, a trip Michael has his heart set on.

"Mrs. Gebhart? I'm wondering if Michael is still planning on going to Germany with us?"

"What do you mean?" But even as I ask this question, I know the answer.

"Well, the trip fee is due next week and you have yet to pay anything toward it." She seems surprised I don't know, but I assure her I will have the money.

Back in the truck, I whip my cell phone out of my pocket. I know better, but I can't help myself. I call Chet.

"You seriously didn't pay for Michael's trip? He's been planning for a year!" I'm screeching but I don't care.

"The trip is not a necessity, Lorinda."

I can't believe what I'm hearing. "Oh, I see, but gambling away all of our money in Vegas is?" My voice is shaking, my hands are shaking, and still, I can't stop yelling.

If I could reach through the phone and strangle him, I would. I scream until my voice is hoarse and he's long since hung up. I sit in the truck, exhausted from my tirade, and cry. I don't know what I'm going to do or how, but I must come up with thirty-two hundred dollars for Michael's trip in three days. I push the truck into drive and head for home. I need gas again. This monster of a truck constantly needs gas—another thing I'm furious with Chet about. He drives the Mercedes everywhere while I lug children, groceries, and the like in this big gray beast. The stupid thing is probably costing me more than it's worth. I'd be better off without it. And then it hits me: I'll sell the truck.

Sandy shakes her head when I explain what happened at Michael's school. By now, she isn't shocked Chet hasn't paid, as it's just one more thing on a growing list of obligations he's shunned. She checks the Kelly Blue Book price online and says I should try to sell it for thirty-five hundred dollars. I'm desperate, so I post the huge gray truck on Craigslist with photos, and hope for the best.

I'm getting ready to teach cycling class the following morning when I remember to check my listing online. To my delight and relief, someone is interested! I call and set up a meeting in the parking lot of the gym for later in the morning. I can't believe my good fortune and run next door to tell Sandy.

"Lorinda, this is fabulous!" She wraps me in a hug. "I'll write up a contract and help with the transaction if you'd like." I'm grateful to have her help, relieved everything is working out.

I park the truck in a spot that will be easy to get in and out of. If the man shows up while I'm teaching class, Sandy will take care of the sale for me. Sandy heads into the gym, but I run back to the truck to be sure I have everything. Someone calls my name and I freeze. Slowly I turn and see Chet marching across the parking lot.

"That truck it half mine!" He stops within a couple inches of my face. "You've taken everything! I want half of the money from that truck!"

He's using his most intimidating voice, but I know selling the truck is my only shot at getting the money for Michael's trip, he's not going to stand in my way. I don't give him the satisfaction of a response. Instead, I twirl on my heel, walking away as he flings accusations and insults at my back. I push open the gym door, and from the look on my face, Sandy can tell something is wrong. Chet doesn't follow me into the gym but stalks back to the truck where he seems determined to stay until the buyer shows up. Without a word, Sandy grabs the file with the contract she's written and goes out to stand on the other side of the truck. I have to start class before the buyer shows. Silently, I pray everything will work out in my favor. As soon as I end my class, I rush to find Sandy. She stands, holding a fistful of money in her hand and a satisfied smile across her face. To my relief, Chet is nowhere to be found.

Monday morning, I walk into German class and hand Michael's teacher thirty-two hundred dollars.

"Michael will be going on the trip," I say with a smile, and she thanks me.

In the parking lot, I climb on my bike, and despite the hills and the chill of the morning, I barely feel the effort, I'm riding high on my triumph.

Robin and I remain in frequent contact, texting and calling after our reunion at Barnes and Noble. And, in the beginning, I'm beyond ecstatic to be found by her. Yet, the fear Chet will discover us lingers too close to the surface for us to risk meeting in person. But now Chet and I are no longer together, and I fear he'll use Robin as confirmation of his version of the breakup of our marriage. He's made a habit of arbitrarily driving by my rental house, leaving me continually on edge. I'm beginning to understand his personality is such that he may no longer want me, but that doesn't mean he wants anyone else to have me, either. His jealousy continues to rage, I'm wary of fanning the flame. Even still, I won't keep away from Robin forever, not now that I'm free to see her. We decide to meet on a day I believe Chet has gone south to his girlfriend's house.

I watch for Robin's plum-colored truck through the sheer curtains of my living room. When I see her pull up, I grab my fleece vest and run out to meet her. I climb into the cab; Robin leans over and pecks me on the cheek.

"Howdy, darlin'." She puts the truck in gear. "Where do you want to go?"

I shrug, lean back into the seat. Dried lavender bunches cram the visors, a discarded flannel shirt and empty paper Starbucks cups litter the floor.

"Are you living in here?"

She chuckles, snags a sock lying between us and tosses it over her shoulder.

"Practically," she replies. "I've been working full-time at Starbucks and evenings delivering pizzas for Domino's."

She's always been far too generous with her money, but never saved a penny for herself. She lives more paycheck-to-paycheck than I do. The woman she currently lives with has a young son and teenage daughter, all three of whom she helps support. She also sends money to an ex in Idaho who's caring for the horses and dogs they shared. Therefore, at nearly fifty years old, she still has little to call her own.

She swings Purple Rain into the Pier One Imports parking lot; I feel a twinge of nostalgia. When we were still naïve enough to dream of a life together, we wandered through the store picking out our future household décor. The scents, the textures, all seemingly exotic and chic, now appear junky. The overwhelming scent of cheap mango and pineapple candles makes my head hurt. I maneuver around the floor of littered, neon, plastic patio furniture. Robin stops in front of a huge bin of table settings, rifles through the mess. She pulls out an oversized bejeweled napkin ring, pushes it onto my ring finger.

"Marry me!" she laughs. I laugh, too.

The ring twirls comically around my finger, finally sliding off and hitting the floor. Robin scoops it up, chucks it back onto the pile. But when she turns to look at me again, her smile is faded.

"Seriously, though, why can't we be together?"

I think about all the times I've dreamed of nothing else. Now here she is standing right in front of me, and the moment I was sure would never happen, has happened. I'm no longer married. I take her hand, will her to understand what I can't articulate. She squeezes back, but I sense the shift in her mood.

We climb somberly back into her truck. I suggest we drive through Starbucks, because if there is one place in which Robin would gladly stretch out a cot and move into, it's Starbucks. We pull up to the window, Robin rambles off a complicated order. I ask for my usual latte. Sitting next to her, my hands wrapped around my steaming cup, I drift back to the first time I experienced coffee. It had been with Robin, just like so many other firsts. I'm slowly coming to realize that the impressionable young woman I was in my twenties, the one who hung on Robin's every word and fantasized about running off and creating the perfect life together, has now matured under the weight of maternal and marital responsibilities. I no longer feel free to risk being reckless with my heart or hers. I'm searching for stability that will fortify me for the future. I lean over, kiss her on the cheek. She smiles. We part on an upbeat note, but I feel the burden of her disappointment.

Sandy receives and reads Chet's email, along with everyone else in the world. She says she understands why exposing my affair with Robin drove me to feel suicidal, how traumatizing it is to be outed. After pulling me from the cliff, she is especially kind. I appreciate her gentleness; I feel safe in her presence. Since moving next door to her, we have spent more and more time together. We go to dinner, to movies, and for long walks. I'm buffered by her strength, humbled by her generosity, and I've fallen for her smile. I genuinely enjoy her attention, but I'm hypercritical of my motives. Sandy is a divorce lawyer, exactly who I need right now. Her legal counsel and representation are the only factors keeping me afloat in my ongoing court battles with Chet. I worry that maybe my feelings for her aren't authentic.

On June 16, 2012, as the emerald waves lap at the sides of the ferry, Sandy and I travel toward Vancouver Island in Canada. Tofino, British Columbia—far enough from everything, and everyone, she assures me, to feel like a real getaway. I need a getaway. I feel as if I'm in a battle with Chet every moment of every day. He doesn't want to pay child support, he doesn't want to drive two hours north to our hometown to visit his children; he wants them delivered to him at his new address. He hassles me to split belongings we once owned in common that I now use to furnish our rental house. He harasses the boys for "secret" information about me. He's exhausting, and I look forward to the day he just leaves us alone. I know it will come. Michael and Taylor are spending the weekend with Chet, which doesn't promote feelings of ease within. Even now I hold my breath, hoping that all will go well.

On the ferry to Tofino, the sun shines like hundreds of flickering lights across the water, while my mind wanders back to the memory of my eighteen-year-old self exactly twenty-one years ago.

I'm on the Canadian side of the border, changing my clothes in the bathroom. I wonder if my husband-to-be will make it to the wedding on time. He and his friends spent the night in Vancouver for his bachelor party, and have yet to turn up. I step into a calf-length white dress, more appropriate for a high school dance than a wedding, suck in my stomach. I run my hands nervously up and down my waist, hoping I don't look fat. I pull on the flats I've chosen so as not to be taller than Chet, and take care not to run my white tights. My sister, Jennifer, hands me a plastic bouquet holder filled with fraying, pink fabric roses I found at the

Goodwill store. The only real flowers will be those in the park gardens, which are plentiful, in an array of magnificent colors. The day is windy but not unpleasant, and occasionally the clouds adjust to reveal the sun. My family and friends crowd together on the lawn laughing, talking, reuniting with one another. As Jennifer and I make our way across the lawn to the cobblestone steps where the ceremony will take place, we are distracted by the sound of laughing and whooping. Hurdling over the grassy hillside, like the Von Trapp singers from *The Sound of Music*, appear five teenage boys in black suits. They're winded, glowing with perspiration. They swing into position, straightening their clothes as they line up. From a borrowed boom box, my worn tape of Sheriff's sappy eighties ballad, "When I'm with You," crackles to life. Jennifer hands me off to Dad, and his grip tightens around my arm. He's less than thrilled I'm getting married; his disapproval makes me uneasy. I hate the thought of disappointing my dad. I search the crowd gathered at the bottom of the stairs. Mom stands next to Chet's mom, her hands clasped under her chin, her eyes brimming with tears. In contrast to Dad, she couldn't be happier. At eighteen, I'm caught in a flurry of emotion, barely comprehending what being married will genuinely entail.

Now, standing beside Sandy, I watch seals bark and splash alongside the ferry to the delight of the passengers. I'm brought back by the commotion. How different this day is compared to twenty years ago. I lean against the railing, the wind picks up my hair, blows it across my eyes. I sweep it away, lean over a bit farther to watch as the seals' bodies disappear, then reemerge as they glide below the water's surface. Suddenly the ferry lurches, knocks me off balance, but I feel strong arms close around me from behind, steadying me.

"You doing okay?" Sandy asks.

I nod.

Her body shields mine from the chilly breeze coming off the water, I lean into her. Her breath on my neck sends a different kind of chill down my spine. When the ferry heaves to a stop against the bumpers, we follow the other passengers down the stairs, back to our car. We slowly follow the snaking line of automobiles onto one of the island's main highways. Sandy drives us across the island to a cabin nestled in among towering trees. The lime green door and brightly contrasting orange trim give the little cottage a whimsical feel. The charm continues inside with warm, cherrywood cupboards filled with oversized coffee mugs, wine glasses, and cheerfully mismatched dishware. We fill the fridge with food we've brought, and then I explore the rest of the cabin. The shower is outside on the deck without a wall or a curtain to hide behind. I run my fingers along my ribcage, wondering if I'll be brave enough to use it. Alongside the woodstove, rows of books and an eclectic selection of movies line hanging shelves. A queen-size bed dominates the bedroom, the nightstands on either side nothing more than slivers of wood. I pick the side farthest from the door and unpack my clothes.

Sandy grills salmon for dinner that we eat as we sip glasses of wine on the deck. I lay my head back against the deck chair, close my eyes. I laugh to myself. If anyone had told me I'd be spending what would have been my twenty-first wedding anniversary divorcing Chet, and relaxing on an island with a lesbian lawyer I'd met in gym class, I never would have believed them. After refilling my wine glass, Sandy stretches out on the lounge chair next to me.

"How do you feel?" She lifts her glass to her lips.

The wind blows softly through the trees, I take a sip of wine.

"Free," I reply.

We lay quietly listening to the waves as they rush in and crash on the beach below. I can't remember a time when my mind has been so quiet.

"Should we go to bed?" Sandy asks.

The sun has disappeared, the air has grown cool. I nod and she helps me stand up. I'm tipsy. I giggle as I sway on my feet. Sandy holds me around the waist to steady me, leans in, and kisses me. She guides us into the cabin to the bedroom. We sink into the bed and I don't resist when she pulls open my shirt. The way her skin feels against mine, her breath on my neck, I can't help but draw her closer to me.

twenty-two

The trip to Tofino strengthens me and helps me identify my feelings for Sandy, which is a significant step toward embracing my identity. Expressing my true self is also enormously freeing. Suddenly, I want to stake an equality sign in my yard and scream out loud, "I'm gay!" But this is new territory for me and I'm prone to tripping over my newfound rainbow. Luckily, I have Sandy to guide me. And having her live next door affords our relationship the luxury of unfolding organically. Our separate living quarters are especially beneficial for Michael and Taylor. They continue to have their private space, as well as ample alone time with me at home. Of course, now that they're teenagers, they enjoy me leaving the house to them. Overall, our lives are calmer and more relaxed, and I'm content with our arrangement. But being gay with Sandy is one thing, and being gay around Mom is quite another. I haven't worked up the nerve to come clean with her yet. She doesn't have the internet, so she hasn't read the outing letter from Chet. Nor does she believe him when he calls her to tell her I'm gay. I know I can't put off telling her forever. Aimee knows how heavily this secret is weighing me down, but she also understands how terrified I am to reveal it. Her mom and mine are also best friends, so we have all spent a good deal of time together, and for this reason, Aimee is the one person I feel can help me. A few months after Tofino, we discuss ideas about when and where the revealing should take place. We finally concur that the safest place is probably the upcoming craft and antique fair.

On the day of the fair, we wind in and out of displays of hand-poured candles and thick blocks of earthy-scented soap interspersed with antique tablecloths and doilies. This is a familiar, comfortable place to all of us, and our spirits are light and easy—everyone's but mine, that is. I'm waiting for a bomb to drop as Aimee and I plot via secret text messages and whispers behind our moms' backs. By noon, I'm a nervous wreck and Aimee decidedly takes the reins. She tells my mom she needs to use the ladies' room and asks if she'd care to go with her. My mom agrees, but before Aimee's mom can chime in, Aimee gives me a look I interpret as "Quick, steer her towards jewels!" because if anything can distract her, this will do the trick. Linda's passion for jewelry rivals my love of coffee, and I worship coffee.

"Oh, look at this lovely emerald bracelet!" I croon. Linda turns her attention to the bright bangle I've slipped onto my wrist.

"I love it!" Her eyes widen as she peers closer at the gleaming jewels.

My heart is pounding through my chest as I wait for a sign that Aimee has broken the news to my mom. Finally, after what feels like hours rather than minutes, I spot Aimee's blonde hair bobbing in the distance. She's running in my direction and immediately I know something is wrong. I search the crowd behind her and see Mom's back disappear through the glass doors. I yank the bracelet off my wrist and drop it back onto the display table. I run for the doors and bolt for the parking lot just as Mom's van pulls away.

As soon as I get home, I call my parents' house. Dad answers right away. He's upset because Mom's hysterical.

"Can I talk to her?"

"She's locked herself in her room," he says, and sighs.

My whole life, all I've ever wanted is to please my mom, to feel her adoration and approval, to revel in our similarities. And now, I've devastated her, destroyed our relationship.

"Hello." Her voice is thick with tears and exhaustion.

"Mom, I'm so sorry—"

"I will never accept this," she hollers with unexpected gusto. "The thought is disgusting and makes my stomach turn."

I'm too stunned to respond, even though I know this is exactly what I deserve.

"When your husband called and told us about you," she continues, "I didn't believe him but . . ." She clucks her tongue. "Lorinda, you know better."

It's the same age-old admonishment she has used for years, but this time I feel a layer tear away from my heart, exposing decades of raw, long-suppressed rage. I erupt in retaliation.

"My being a lesbian does not justify what Chet has done to me and our kids. You have no idea what I've been through," I shriek. "The years I've poured into studying the Bible. The church programs I've attended. And therapy . . . So. Much. Therapy. I can't change!"

"The Bible is clear. I know what I believe," Mom quips, not inclined to give in.

"You believe what you've been told!" I bite back. "You have no desire to learn. You're a robot. And running off like a child is unacceptable," I continue. "When you want to talk to me like an adult, you know where to find me."

I've never raised my voice to my mother before. I immediately regret it, but I don't apologize. My filter has disappeared. Instead, I slam down the phone. Soon, my whole body is shaking and the only comfort I find is in cocooning myself inside my quilt and crying myself to sleep. In my dreams, Mom wraps me in her arms, tells me how much she loves me, and apologizes for all the years I struggled in silence living as someone I'm not.

In reality, aside from a cordial hello and goodbye at the gym, she quits talking to me.

Several months after falling out with my mother, our relationship has yet to improve, although I cannot say it has grown worse either. We have come to an impasse, and I'm trying to be okay with that. But a deep loneliness has settled in and around me because I don't know how to live without my mom. Yet, I feel certain she can only love the daughter she thought I was, the one she wants me to be. The real me, the authentic me, will never be good enough.

I've been nursing a cold for over a week and I feel crappy. Draped in a blanket and burrowed into a ball in the corner of my couch, my one and only goal for the evening is not to move. I hear my phone buzz, but I close my eyes and ignore it. It buzzes again. When it buzzes a third time, I snatch it from the arm of the couch. A text from Sandy flashes across the screen. She wants me to get dressed and meet her on the porch of her house. *No, no, no.* I cover my face with my blanket. I live close enough to reach my hand through my living room window and touch Sandy through hers, but now she seems too far away. My sinuses drain down the back of my throat. The phone rings. *Shit.* I answer.

"Hey, did you get my text?" Sandy's breathless, excited.

"Oh, no, sorry," I lie, sniffling with noticeable intensity, in case she's forgotten I'm sick.

"Come over," she orders. "I'm taking you to dinner!"

My mind sprints to work up a protest, but Sandy's already hung up. I lumber to my feet.

"I don't like real clothes," I grumble, grabbing jeans and a sweater. I feel like shit, I look like shit. There's no way I'm fit for going out. I'll simply have to convince Sandy this isn't going to happen tonight. Still, I glance in the mirror as I pass hoping to find I've miraculously transformed into a super model. I haven't. I get one foot on the first step to Sandy's porch when she bursts through the door, darts down the stairs past me.

"How are you feeling?" she chirps, opening the passenger door of her car for me.

"Not great." I cough, but Sandy only smiles wider.

"I'll get you a hot drink," she promises. "You'll feel better in no time!"

I climb into the passenger seat, lean my head back. Though it's not uncommon for Sandy to spontaneously take me out, it is uncommon for her not to pick up the cues I'm so obviously sending her. Sandy has made no mention as to where we're going, and frankly, I'm in no mood to ask. If I had to guess, I'd say we're headed to Skylarks. She took me there on our first date about a year ago, and since then, it's become one of our favorite restaurants. We've even become friends with a specific waiter, John, who waited on us our first night and every time since.

We pull into a parking spot, and Sandy hops out of the car. She opens my door, holds her hand out to me. The feel of her hand wrapped firmly around mine sends an exhilarating jolt through my body. I lift my head a little higher as we walk into the restaurant, hand in hand. Sandy gives the hostess our names and she sits us at a table against the wall close to the fireplace. I drop into my chair, wrestling my arms free of my bulky jacket.

"Good evening, ladies." John appears with two glasses of Riesling. "Will we be enjoying the usual?" he asks, setting wine down in front of us. He pulls the menus from under his arm, swings them back and forth.

We nod, thank him. He tucks the menus back under his arm, heads toward the kitchen. I'm grateful not to have to make any decisions.

Sandy holds her glass to mine; we clink them gently. "To us!" she declares and we both take a sip.

The alcohol slides easily down my throat, instantly helping me relax. We chat about nothing and everything in the easy manner I've grown to value with her. For so long, I lived weighted down under a yoke of lies about who I believed I was, who I believed I should be, and who I truly longed to be. But here, sitting across from a successful lesbian lawyer, being waited on by an openly gay waiter, I'm keenly aware of the unbelievable turn my life has taken. I'm finally with my people, living the life I've longed for. I can't help but feel overwhelmed with gratitude, and I nearly forget my earlier crankiness.

After we finish our meals, I push away my empty plate. I've never been someone who finds it impossible to eat when I'm sick; I can eat my way through any illness. John returns to the table to collect our dishes and places a steaming mug of hot buttered rum in front of me.

"I didn't order this—" I start to say, but Sandy cuts me off.

"Thank you, John." She winks. He winks back.

I narrow my eyes suspiciously at Sandy. I tilt the mug, attempt to inhale, through my partially stuffed nose, the scents of nutmeg, brown sugar, and rum I know are there. I can't help but laugh out loud as I think of a scene in a movie featuring the actor Ryan Reynolds. I hold up my mug and recite, "It's like Christmas in a cup!"

Sandy and I both exclaim, "*The Proposal!*" at the same time, and laugh. Then she reaches across the table, takes my hands in hers. She clears her throat, looks into my eyes.

"Speaking of *The Proposal*..." She releases my hands.

My body suddenly feels dangerously light. I wrap my fingers around the seat of my chair to hold myself down. She pulls a blue box tied in a white satin bow from her jacket pocket, slides it across the table. I remain fixed in place.

"Open it," she coaxes, with a nervous chuckle. But I can't move. "Open it," she insists.

I bring one hand to the table, tug gently at the ribbon. Sandy lifts the lid, exposing the largest, shiniest, most perfect diamond ring I've ever seen. She pulls it out, holds it delicately between her forefinger and thumb.

"Lorinda . . ."

I take in a deep breath and hold it, marveling at the gravity of what's about to happen. My whole life has been leading to this one moment. The moment when I declare to the world, to Sandy, and most importantly, to myself, that I'm in love with a woman and she is in love with me.

"Lorinda," Sandy repeats, "will you marry me?"

I exhale slowly, willing myself not to cry. "Yes," I shout, "yes, I will marry you." I lean in, my face wet with happy tears and we kiss.

She slides the diamond onto my finger.

"Whew," she laughs, pretending to wipe the sweat from her brow.

A gust of wind blows through the restaurant as the door opens and our friends Dina and Gary enter. I laugh as I imagine them outside, faces pressed up against the windows waiting for a sign that all has gone as planned. They wrap us in hugs and shower us with congratulations.

John appears again, balancing a tray on the tips of his fingers. "Congratulations!" he says, setting a glass of champagne in front of each of us. We toast and cheer, and I completely forget about my cold.

I spend the night at Sandy's house filled to the brim with love, exhilaration, and wine. I can't imagine my life being any more perfect. But my moment of clarity is short-lived.

The next day, as I sit drinking coffee in Sandy's kitchen, staring blindly out the window, I find myself once again questioning whether I'm marrying her for the right reasons. Even before we officially began dating, she was so certain of her love for me, so positive I was the one that she had her will changed to include me in it. But after she's waited her whole life for the right to legally marry, I want to be sure I'm worthy of the wait.

Seemingly sensing my hesitancy, Sandy lays her hand on my shoulder, and I turn to face her. "You deserve a good life, Lorinda. You deserve to be happy and those who absolutely love you will want that for you, too."

Oh, how I want to believe her. I want to imagine everyone in my life falling into line and happily rooting for my new life. But I think of my parents, and specifically, Mom, and my confidence wanes. So, for now, Sandy and I agree to stretch out the wedding planning, giving me time to adjust and hopefully finding a way to tell Mom. I know that I don't want Mom to hear about my engagement to Sandy from anyone other than me. I've already hurt her, and I so long for the love we shared before she knew I was gay. Before I disgusted her. Before, when I was still her perfect daughter.

twenty-three

On February 13, 2012, just four months after Sandy's proposal, Governor Christine Gregoire signs legislation that establishes full marriage rights for same-sex couples in the state of Washington. Jumping up and down in Sandy's living room, we take in the amazing news. We won't have to travel to another state or country to marry. Instead, we can marry right here, in our own city. The excitement we feel leads us to begin planning our wedding in earnest. We decide on October of the same year—2013—and I push from my mind the fact that I've yet to tell Mom.

Telling my kids is difficult in a different way as I realize the finality it puts on the life we shared with Chet. Never again will we be our original family of four. Michael and Taylor both reassure me that I deserve to be happy. They like Sandy and think I should marry her. But despite their brave faces, I see pain in their eyes, the demise of their parents' marriage has not left them unscathed. I turn to Aimee and Jerrie for reassurance that I'm doing the right thing. They both agree that if I'm happy, my children will be, too. Aimee and Jerrie remind me of the anguish I've endured to get to this place in my life. But even their buffering can't totally erase my uneasiness. Some days I feel more confident and search Pinterest for wedding ideas; other days I consider telling Sandy we need to call the whole thing off. This volleying of emotions eventually takes a toll. One night, I break down in a total state of despair.

Sandy wraps her arms around me. "This isn't something we have to do any specific time. We can wait until you are ready." She kisses the top of my head.

The thing is, I want to marry her, but just below the surface of my newfound freedom, I still fear God will knock me down. After all, I've been raised to trust the Bible is the literal, inspired Word of God. And I've yet to shake the condemnation I feel as I habitually recite verses in my head that I learned as a child. Leviticus 18:22: "Thou shalt not lie with mankind, as with womankind: it is an abomination." Leviticus 20:13: "If a man also lies with mankind, as he lieth with a woman, both of them have committed an abomination: they shall surely be put to death." These words come as easily as my own name and I have no idea how to drown them out. Revelation 21:8 reads: "But as for the cowardly, the faithless, the detestable, as for murderers, the sexually immoral, sorcerers, idolaters, and all liars, their portion will be in the lake that burns with fire and sulfur, which is the second death." This verse clearly states that if I don't repent, turn from my evil ways, I'll burn for eternity in Hell. For this reason alone, I know Mom will never change her mind about me. What kind of mother would she be if she turned her head, condoned behavior condemning me to Hell forever?

What I have yet to embrace is that many people do not believe in what I've been taught. There are plenty of people who think exactly as I did as a young child, that the Bible is simply a collection of stories. That, yes, some of the messages can be picked apart and applied to life today, but that most are old fables meant to serve people at a different time in history.

In June, seven months after I've accepted Sandy's proposal of marriage, I get a call from my cousin, Tommy. He and I have corresponded infrequently on Facebook but haven't spoken in years. He, too, has endured the same strict fundamentalist Christian upbringing as I, but the difference is, he got out. He moved away from our family, from our home state, and all that held him under the thumb of religious guilt. Recently, I was bold enough to post a picture of Sandy and me in front of a rainbow flag on my Facebook page. We're each holding up a pair of socks we purchased at a local store after the Bellingham Pride Parade a week earlier. Both say "bride." My parents don't have computers, so I figure by now, the people I still associate with from my "straight" life know I'm gay. But it's this picture that prompts a call from Tommy.

"So ya'll getting married, then?" he drawls.

"Yes!" I shout back. I don't mean to, but my excitement at being able to share with another gay person bubbles over.

"Good for you!" he squeals happily. "And how's the folks takin' it?" I hear him click his tongue as if he already knows the answer.

The joy we shared a moment earlier now dissipates into a dark cloud. I imagine Mom locking herself in her bedroom again, crying herself into sickness because I'm marrying a woman.

"So, not good?" Tommy's voice breaks through.

"I haven't actually told them," I admit, then I begin to cry.

"Oh, honey," he says, and sighs. "That religion we learned as kids is total shit. There ain't nobody gonna strike you down. *Girl,* you live your life and be happy, ya hear?"

He understands where I come from. He knows our family, our faith. In a rush and through my tears, I spill my guts, dump years of anguish on him. I tell him about Robin, my divorce from Chet, the confrontation with Mom, and Sandy's spectacular proposal. Tommy listens, and when I've poured it all out, I hear him sigh again.

"I didn't know." He sounds sad, as if he's sorry he wasn't there for me sooner. But this one call, this one connection with someone from my family, from my old world, matters more to me than he realizes. He gives me something, someone, to hang on to. He has made a life for himself, and I will, too. Before we hang up, we promise to keep in touch.

By the end of September, our wedding plans have come together. We will be married at the Squalicum Boathouse alongside the bay. The building is a natural wood construction designed with an oversized fireplace in a large room, perfect for guests to gather in. My cousin, Deanne, volunteers to bake our wedding cake and cupcakes, and our friend Penny offers to make me a wedding dress. My lifelong girlfriends come together to set up tables and chairs, to decorate, and even to do my hair.

Less than a month before our wedding is set to take place, I still haven't worked up the courage to tell Mom it's happening, let alone invite her. Each time I see her at the gym, I try to work my news into casual conversation, but it's difficult now. Mom and I speak only in short, clipped phrases. But one morning after class ends, I stop her on her way to her car. I wait until we're in the parking lot, no one within earshot. At first, she says nothing, and then she lets out a long, pained sigh.

"I don't think we can come." She averts her eyes to the ground. "You should be able to enjoy the day," she mumbles.

I nod, wait, hope for more. For a confirmation that we're okay despite this, despite the obvious fact that I've disappointed her. But I'm not going to get anything more. I've failed as her daughter, and my wedding announcement has as much as finalized this truth. She leans in, embraces me in an awkward hug, then gets in her car and drives away. I didn't expect her to be happy for me, but I hadn't prepared for how badly her rejection would hurt, either. I remain standing in the parking lot several minutes after she's gone, unable to decide what to do next. The familiar sting of tears threatens to further diminish my composure, and eventually, I decide to return to the gym, gather my things, and go home.

Sandy takes my parents' decision not to attend in stride, but I know she's hurt. Sandy believes she's more than proven to my parents her love and dedication for me, and though I try to explain to her that Mom's condemnation only comes from the fact that we're both women, she can't help but take Mom's refusal personally. Especially since Sandy's elderly parents would give anything to attend if her father were well enough to travel from Wisconsin to Washington.

After my encounter with Mom, I'm reluctant to invite my family at all. Of course, my cousin, Jerrie, and her family will attend. I've never doubted their support. But I'm uncertain as to whether I should ask my sister. Then, to my relief, Jennifer approaches me to let me know she will be coming. I'm both relieved and buffered to know she'll be there. Aside from my own children, Jerrie's family, and Jennifer, the only other relatives of mine to attend are my cousin, Lisa, and her husband, Vern. They make the two-hour drive from Seattle to attend, which warms my heart. Any misgivings I might have had about who else I should invite proves unnecessary. My core group of lifelong friends demonstrate that they're much more accepting than our conservative upbringing led me to imagine. Not only are they eager to attend, they also offer to assist in whatever way they can. As my list of guests begins to round out, I feel more confident. Then Aimee tells me her mom, Linda, and her aunts want to be invited. Though I'm truly touched they want to support me, I can't help but wonder how Mom will react—and she will find out. She and Linda are best friends. But Aimee convinces me everything will be fine, so I agree to invite her mom and her aunts.

October 5, 2013, is an ideal Pacific Northwest weather day. Burnt orange, fire red, and sun yellow leaves carpet the landscape, a mild breeze carries the scent of salt from across the bay. The sun shines from a clear blue sky stretching its rays through the windows of the boathouse, warming the shoulders of our guests. Sandy and I stand together just outside the door waiting for our friend, Hannah, to signal us in to begin the ceremony. The excitement I feel, combined with my nerves, leaves me trembling, but Sandy slips her arm around my waist and holds me tightly, reassuringly. The buzz of conversation from inside the building quiets, and Hannah smiles, waves her hand at us. I take in a deep breath, and as I look up, ready to take my first steps toward the altar, my eyes come directly in contact with Aimee's. Her eyes fill with tears as she gives me a firm, knowing nod and mouths the words "I love you." I fight back my own tears as I nod back. Mom's best friend, my aunt, and Aimee's aunts beam at Sandy and me. I'm struck with a pang of longing for my own mother, but so grateful for these women, these chosen mothers, who are here to bear witness on this most important day in my life.

Sandy and I have written our own vows and speak them to each other with profound emotion. Sandy's first words to me are "You are enough," and with her, I understand that I am. Not only am I enough, but I'm also exactly, perfectly who and where I'm meant to be. I'm authentically me. Hannah pronounces us married, and Sandy and I kiss. We throw our arms up in celebration, and the entire room erupts in applause and cheering. We make our way around the room, hugging and thanking our guests. Sandy and I dance to "Make You Feel My Love," as sung by Adele, and once the song concludes, my uncle David, Jerrie's dad, takes my hand.

"I must dance with my niece on her wedding day," he says, and without missing a beat, he pulls me into step. His thoughtful gesture fills me with gratitude as I acknowledge how he's filled in for my own father without any prompting.

Before midnight, we have the building cleared and cleaned, and Sandy and I are off to spend the night at the nearby Hotel

Bellwether. We fall into bed, exhausted, exuberant, and most amazingly, married.

"I love you, Sandy," I say, as she balances over me on the bed.

"We are going to have a beautiful life together," she replies, bringing her lips toward mine.

twenty-four

Two months after we wed, Sandy and I buy a home, fulfilling her promise I'll never be homeless again. With our three sons and various pets in tow, we settle into a remodeled, hundred-year-old farmhouse, complete with a barn, potting shed, huge garden, and even a gazebo with a cookstove we plan to use for marshmallow roasting. By April, the warmer weather makes it possible for me to get outside and garden. Though surrounded by six acres, only about an acre of the property is landscaped. Of that acre, there are at least two dozen flower beds to be cleaned out, as well as a large vegetable garden behind the house in need of tilling. If I let myself ponder the immensity of work to be done, I'm sent into anxiety overdrive. I decide to begin in front of the house and attack the beds closest to the porch. About an hour in, I rest my chin on the handle of my shovel, surveying my progress as I sway to the music playing on my cell phone. Suddenly, the song is interrupted by ringing, and the phone nearly vibrates off the upturned bucket I've propped it on. As I pull off my gloves, dirt flies up my nose, and I sneeze.

"Hello?" I cradle the phone in the crook of my neck.

"Lorinda, it's Dad. Your Aunt Gayle has died. Your mother needs you. We're at Gayle's apartment."

I pull the phone away from my ear. Sweat trickles down my neck. The hairs on my arms raise as if I've just stepped into an air-conditioned building. *Died?*

I recall Mom informing me that Gayle was terminally ill with ovarian cancer, that my favorite auntie was slipping away. Fifteen years earlier, her husband left her, and Aunt Gayle was unable to overcome her husband's betrayal. No matter what anyone said or did, she continued to decline in health and in spirit. In the beginning, I tried to rally her, to encourage her via phone calls, cards, and letters, but my immaturity and my limited experience in the cruelties of life left me impatient and not nearly compassionate enough. Eventually, I drifted away. Now, the similarities between the way Chet left me and the way my uncle left my aunt are not lost on me. I allow the profound feelings of betrayal and loss over the demise of my twenty-year marriage to Chet to rise to the surface. I ache for the teenage love that did not last, for the family unit my children lost. But then I let the emotions pass.

I call to Sandy, explain what's happened. She offers to drive me to my aunt's apartment. My heart races at the thought of seeing Mom in such a vulnerable situation. We haven't been close in some time, and I'm uncertain she'll want to see me at all.

We pull into the parking lot where Sandy parks next to Mom's van. "Honey, I'll wait for you in the car," Sandy says. She leans over and gives me a quick hug.

Mom is wrapped in Dad's arms; he looks up when he sees me. I tentatively touch my hand to Mom's back; she turns to face me. I pull her into me. She sobs and I cry along with her. The cold wind blows hard against us. I'm struck with the unceremonious way in which two men carry Aunt Gayle's body down two flights of stairs and roll it into the back of a minivan. As they drive off, Mom's grip on my hand is almost painful. Here we are again, Mom and me. Just five years earlier, Mom had pressed her head into my shoulder and cried helplessly as my grandmother's ashes were lowered into the ground. Watching her suffer as she lost her mom, and now, her sister, breaks my heart. As the oldest child, I feel a great sense of responsibility for her, for Dad. I recognize she's too fragile to drive, so I offer to drive her home in her van. Dad's already left in his truck. I stick my head through the window of my car, let Sandy know my plans. She agrees to follow me to my parents' house.

As I drive, I can't help but feel the chasm between Mom and me. Since I married Sandy, Mom and I continue to talk nearly every day at the gym when she comes to class, but our conversations are on the surface. We are pleasant enough, but I long for more. I desperately miss hanging out for hours, thumbing through home decorating magazines, taking long walks while chatting about everything under the sun, or even meandering aimlessly through Target together. I miss my mom.

I walk her up the stairs of her house and I frantically grab for her hand.

"That could have been you in that body bag today," I choke. "What would it matter, then, Mom, if I were gay or straight? I'm still me."

"You've changed, Lorinda. You may not see it, but you have. I'll never accept you being gay." She's shaking, tears slide down her cheeks.

"Then don't. But don't shut me out either," I beg.

With that, she folds me into her arms and sobs into my shoulder.

One week after Aunt Gayle's funeral, six months after marrying Sandy, and four months after moving into our new house, Mom pulls into my driveway for the first time. I peer cautiously through the curtained window, watch her make her way up the steps to my front door. I open on the first knock, and Mom thrusts a pot of sunshine daffodils and purple hibiscus under my nose. I accept the potted plant, motion for her to come in. She steps inside and immediately wraps me in a hug.

"Oh, Lorinda." Her arms squeeze tightly around me.

I feel instantly relieved and optimistically victorious as I pull away from her embrace.

"Welcome to our home, Mom."

epilogue: robin

During my struggles with Chet and my mom, and my deepening love affair with Sandy, my friendship with Robin remains intact, but strained. Since our meetup at Pier One, we continue to feel the awkwardness left by my inability to answer her question about why we are no longer together.

Even still, we speak almost daily via text message and keep up with each other on social media. When I tell her Sandy and I plan to marry, she's angry, hurt. She cannot grasp me marrying anyone other than her. I don't have what I believe to be an adequate response, so I don't try to explain. I assure her I want her to remain in my life, and ultimately, I hope she wants me in hers, and then I leave room for us to adapt to our new reality. But the news is just too much for her to bear, and we fall out of contact.

Even before I had my first appointment with the Beller, writing was how I made sense of my thoughts. I've filled countless journals and diaries, chronicling life's painfully mundane to extremely significant moments. Now I turn to writing with re-newed vigor in an attempt to navigate my new life. I'm overcome with guilt and sadness for what has become of my relationship with Robin and, at the same time, I look forward to building a new life with Sandy.

During one counseling session, the Beller suggests I may want to begin compiling my writing into a book. I brush her off.

"Lorinda, you are a gifted writer, and I believe your words could really help others." She hauls out a stack of papers she's collected since our initial meeting nearly twenty years earlier. "I couldn't bear to throw them out," she admits with a smile.

I'm flattered. I love to write; I've always dreamed of being an author. Still, writing about my life seems terrifying. Multiple times, I pull out the stack of papers from my desk drawer. I read a page or two and then file them away again. Even if I were to consider a book, I have no idea where or even how to begin.

Then, my cousin, Jerrie, asks if I'd like to join her in a weekly creative writing class at the local community college, and I agree. Our writing instructor is just who I need. She fosters a supportive, nonjudgmental atmosphere in class and enthusiastically encour-ages us to share our writing aloud. But I'm in such total awe of the skill level among my class members, I'm hesitant to share. Several weeks pass before I muster the courage to read one of my pieces aloud. I'm sure my voice is too quiet, too shaky, and that my face burns crimson, but I stumble through. When I've fin-ished reading, my classmates take turns repeating lines or words they especially appreciated. I feel bolstered. After that night, I push myself to keep up the momentum. I try not to let more than a week pass before I share again, and I even begin looking forward to speaking aloud.

"Who was the first person you fell in love with?" asks our writing instructor one evening at the start of class.

"I'm giving you fifteen minutes to write. Go!"

My words tumble effortlessly across the paper. I describe the camping trip where Robin and I kissed for the first time. My whole body burns with excitement as I pour out this very personal love story I've held in my heart. I decide not to share with the group that night. Instead, I tuck my notebook away. At home, I type out my piece on my laptop. I read it over and over, and each time, I feel strongly about what I must do. So, without giving myself a chance to chicken out, I email it to Robin. I'm not sure she will even respond, and I think I could maybe be okay with that. What I can no longer live with is this feeling that I've never honestly told her how much she means to me.

Two days later, she calls.

"You read it?"

"I did," she replies.

"And?" I wait.

"And . . ." She takes in a deep breath. "I trust you to write our story."

My heart skips.

We pick up from where we left off before I told her about my engagement. We fully reconnect as we discuss the hypothetical book I'll one day write. We even contemplate how the book could end, though we never come to a firm resolution. Our friendship, having veered off onto a path neither of us could have predicted, is once again solid.

Many nights, Robin and I text each other good night before we sign off for the evening, and occasionally, we call. Such is the case the night before Robin's forty-ninth birthday.

"Howdy, darlin'."

I smile at her familiar greeting. "Hey, almost-birthday-girl. You have big birthday plans?"

She chuckles softly, but she sounds weary. "Nah. You tell me about your day."

I rattle on about work and whether I should cut my hair or let it grow long again. I tell her about the car I finally bought because I was tired of being on a first-name basis with the AAA guy.

She chuckles again. "Hey," she cuts in, her voice quiet. "I've always loved you."

"And I've always loved you," I reply.

Robin doesn't make it to forty-nine. She dies that night in her sleep.

The next morning, I receive a call from Hope, my former coworker from Central Services. She and I had reconnected on Facebook over the years, as seems to be the trend, and we've developed a friendship.

"Hey," she says, "Uh, I have to tell you that Robin is . . . gone."

"Gone where?"

"I mean, she died. I wanted to tell you before you read about it on social media."

My mind takes off at full speed as I try to rationalize this information. I can only conclude that Hope is wrong, that she has obviously made a mistake.

I call Robin's number. Her voice breaks in, and I feel waves of hysteria sweeping through my body. I knew it! I knew Hope was wrong.

"Robin!" I yell, screeching into the phone. "I knew you weren't dead!"

But Robin's voice continues in the same even tone as she asks me to please leave a message. I call again, and again, and again, until finally her phone will not accept new messages.

Over Facebook, I learn that her service will be held in a restaurant at the harbor on Bellingham Bay. The manager of the Starbucks store where Robin worked has offered to cater her memorial. Hope kindly offers to attend her memorial with me and I accept gratefully.

The baristas arrive, maybe twelve in all, wearing signature green Starbucks aprons. In the right corner of each apron is a photo button of Robin's smiling face. They bring her apron along, too, splayed out for everyone to see. It's covered front and back in Sharpie-written messages from both adoring coworkers and customers.

Robin's sisters had found and brought along shoeboxes of used Starbucks gift cards Robin had saved and collected over the years, and they lay scattered over the tables in front of the sign, urging people to take one in remembrance. I run the tips of my fingers over them, stopping at one with a drawing of a single coffee cup. I pick it up, hold it in my hands, and rub my thumbs over the image.

"Oh, I don't care for coffee," I say.

"Well then, darlin', maybe you haven't met the right coffee."
She winks.

Eventually, I drop the card back on the table and slowly make my way to where the baristas have gathered to hand out steaming cups of coffee. I inhale the rich smell of coffee beans, watch as the barista whips up steaming milk. I accept a cup of coffee. Hope loops her arm in mine, asks if I'm ready to go. I nod and we start to leave.

At the door, I turn back to gaze one last time at the picture of Robin propped on the table. I take in her bright eyes, feathered with laugh lines, and I feel the same jolt of electricity I felt the first day we met. I lift my coffee cup, give her a wink.

"This one's for you, darlin'."

acknowledgments

There are so many more people who've positively influenced my writing of this memoir and to all of you, thank you, thank you, thank you. Please forgive me for not naming each of you individually, but I hope you know who you are.

Without Michelle Beller-Siegfried, this book dream would never have come to pass. Thank you for holding me up year after year, tragedy after tragedy, and most importantly, for keeping me alive. My cousin and friend Jerrie Minaker-Luginbill talked me into taking our first creative writing class together. Jer, just when we thought we knew everything there was to know about each other, we learned how much more there was yet to uncover, we're just deep like that (Twigs). Thank you for being by my side the entire way. Our creative writing instructor, Nancy Canyon, drew out the stories living inside of us and taught us how to structure them in story format. An accomplished author and artist in her own right, Nancy has a gift for sparking and fueling the creativity within her students. She surely is responsible for lighting that fire in me. Thank you, Nancy. Cami Ostman and The Narrative Project saw me through the development of my story and taught me the value of writing critique in community. Thank you, Cami, for your copious amounts of patience. You know how to talk an author down from her proverbial ledge and you did that for me many times. Through the Narrative Project, Lisa Dailey was assigned to me as my writing beta-buddy, and I won the lottery! We spent hours and hours writing together at our local Barkley Starbucks. Lisa, your camaraderie was game-changing as far as finishing this book was concerned, and I am so grateful to you and to Sidekick Press.

Aimee Wilson, my best friend since preschool, I know you're still mad about my second scoop at the candy game, so I hope that by mentioning my undying love for you in my book, I'll finally be forgiven. You did say you would make an exception and read my memoir even though you don't like to read—I'm holding you to it, BFF.

Raphie, you listened to me blather on about this book day after day, run after run, mile after mile for years and pretended to be interested every time. I love you for every mile, every pep talk.

Al Clover, I'm so fortunate to have you as a longtime client, friend, and writing buddy. You have been one of my most dedicated fans, whether I deserve it or not.

Dad, Mom, Jennifer: my love for you never wavers and never will.

Thank you, Bill Akers, for loving me unconditionally through all the many phases of my life. You mean so much to me.

My fucking-perfect wife, Sandy, without you, this book would not have come to fruition. You are my biggest fan, my cheerleading squad, my partner, lover, and friend. My dear, I carry your heart.

To my kids, Caleb, and Dawson, I love you with all my heart, unconditionally. I hope you will always seek out and live your most authentic lives. I am and always will be so immensely proud of you.

about the author

Lorinda Boyer is a life-long reader and writer. She published an excerpt from *Straight Enough* in *True Stories, The Narrative Project, Volume I* in 2019 and she posts regularly on her blog https://lorindaboyer.com. When she isn't writing, Lorinda works as a personal trainer and fitness instructor and enjoys jogging, hiking, and cycling.

She makes a home with her wife in Tucson, Arizona.

CPSIA information can be obtained
at www.ICGtesting.com
Printed in the USA
LVHW110549060422
715106LV00004B/7